ON THE MISERY OF THE
HUMAN CONDITION · *De miseria*
humane conditionis

The Library of Liberal Arts

LOTHARIO DEI SEGNI
(Pope Innocent III)

ON THE MISERY OF THE HUMAN CONDITION · *De miseria humane conditionis*

Donald R. Howard, Editor
The Johns Hopkins University
Translated by Margaret Mary Dietz

The Library of Liberal Arts
published by
THE BOBBS-MERRILL COMPANY, INC.
Indianapolis · New York

Lothario dei Segni (Pope Innocent III)
1160 (1161)–1216

ACKNOWLEDGMENTS

The Latin text used is Michele Maccarrone (ed.), *Lotharii Cardinalis (Innocentii III) De miseria humane conditionis* (Thesaurus Mundi : Lugano, 1955). Quotations from the Bible are from the Douai-Rheims translation (Douay Bible House: New York, 1944), with a few slight changes made to suit the author's purpose in quoting a passage.

The translator wishes to thank John Waldron and the Rev. James A. McEnerney, S. J. Translator and editor alike are indebted to John P. McCall for his good advice and generous assistance, and to Myra L. Uhlfelder for her close attention to matters of accuracy in the translation. The translation in its earlier unrevised form was presented as a Master's thesis at Georgetown University.

The editor wishes to thank Lynn White, Jr., Morton W. Bloomfield, and John Baldwin for reading the introduction and suggesting many additions and changes.

MARGARET MARY DIETZ
DONALD R. HOWARD

CONTENTS

On the Misery of the Human Condition

BOOK THREE: THE DAMNABLE EXIT FROM THE
HUMAN CONDITION

INTRODUCTION

I · THE SIGNIFICANCE OF THE "DE MISERIA"

The work translated here, for the first time in English since the sixteenth century, was the classic medieval treatment of the "human condition." Written at the close of the twelfth century, it was read throughout Europe for more than four hundred years. It was as much an influence upon Renaissance men as upon their ancestors; even the great treatises of the Italian humanists on the dignity of man mentioned it with respect, offering rebuttals not to prove it wrong but to develop the other side of its argument. Montaigne, often credited with the invention of the phrase *la condition humaine,* undoubtedly knew it. It survives today in nearly 500 manuscripts (an extraordinary number) preserved in libraries of all European nations.[1] It was printed in more than fifty editions before the nineteenth century, the earliest known at Cologne *ca.* 1473, the last in Paris in 1645.[2] It

[1] See Michele Maccarrone, ed., *Lotharii Cardinalis (Innocentii III) De Miseria humane conditionis* (Lugano: Thesaurus Mundi, 1955), pp. x–xx. For other manuscripts see K. V. Sinclair, "Another Manuscript of Lotario's *De miseria,*" and M. Maccarrone, "Altri manoscritti del 'De miseria'," in *Italia Medioevale e umanistica,* IV (1961), 167–173; Donald R. Howard, "Thirty New Manuscripts of Pope Innocent III's *De miseria humane conditionis (De contemptu mundi),*" *Manuscripta,* VII (1963), 31–35; Robert Enzer Lewis, "More New Manuscripts of Pope Innocent III's *De Miseria Humanae Conditionis,*" *Manuscripta,* VIII (1964), 172–175.

[2] Printed editions are listed in Maccarrone, pp. xx–xxii. The Pollard and Redgrave *Short-Title Catalogue* (London, 1926) lists four English editions not mentioned by Maccarrone, issued in London and dated 1576 (two editions in this year), 1577, and 1586. Dr. Franklin B. Williams, Jr., of Georgetown University has pointed out to the translator a previously unknown edition of 1580 now in the British Museum. An undated edition appeared probably in the late 1460's in Germany; see *Catalogue of Books Printed in the XVth Century Now in the British Museum* (London, 1908), III, 707.

was translated into nearly all European languages—even, during the fifteenth century, into Irish.[3] In the seventeenth century it fell into disregard, and has been known only to specialists in medieval studies since then; a good modern edition of it never existed until 1957, when Maccarrone's appeared. To deal with its place in western thought is therefore to deal with the life and death of one of the great books of its age.

In England alone its influence was enormous. Chaucer tells us in the *Legend of Good Women* that he had translated "the Wreched Engendrynge of Mankynde,/ As man may in Pope Innocent yfynde,"[4] but the translation has not survived. (A poem called *An Holy Medytacion* contains parts of Pope Innocent's work, and this appeared in some manuscripts of *The Canterbury Tales,* but the chance that it was Chaucer's has been roundly discredited.)[5] On the other hand, some passages, clearly from the *De miseria,* occur elsewhere in Chaucer's works.[6] Much of the *De miseria* was translated and included in *The Pricke of Conscience,* a late fourteenth-century ascetical treatise of immense popularity in its time.[7] It is quoted once in *Piers Plowman,* and other passages show its influence.[8] In Elizabethan times it

---

[3] *An Irish Version of Innocent III's De contemptu mundi,* ed. James A. Geary (Dissertation, Catholic University, Washington, D.C., 1931).

[4] G-prologue, lines 414–415.

[5] For the controversy on this point see Carleton Brown, *Publications of the Modern Language Association,* L (1935), 997–1011; Beatrice Daw Brown, *Modern Philology,* XXXV (1938), 325–333; Carleton Brown, *Modern Language Notes,* LI (1936), 296–300; Germaine Dempster, *Ibid.,* 284–295, and *Modern Philology,* XXXV (1937), 27–29; J. S. P. Tatlock, *Modern Language Notes,* LI (1936), 275–284.

[6] See John E. Wells, *A Manual of the Writings in Middle English, 1050–1400* (New Haven, Conn.: Yale University Press, 1916), pp. 620, 700–701, 709, 717. See also Robert Enzer Lewis, "Chaucer's Artistic Use of Pope Innocent III's *De miseria humane conditionis* in the Man of Law's Prologue and Tale," *PMLA,* LXXXI (1966), 485–492.

[7] *The Pricke of Conscience,* ed. Richard Morris (Berlin: Philological Society, 1863). See Carleton Brown and Rossell H. Robbins, *The Index of Middle English Verse* (New York: Columbia University Press, 1943), Nos. 1193, 3428. See also Wells, pp. 447–449.

[8] A-text Passus IV, 126–127 (from *De miseria,* III, 18); Prologue, 85–89 and III, 143–154 (II, 4–5); II, 169–171, 222–224 (II, 2, 7); V, 152–155, 189–202 (II, 17); I, 109–116 (II, 31). B-text Passus XVII, 315–350 (I, 17). And see Skeat's note on C. XX. 297.

appeared in two translations, neither of which acknowledged its papal authorship, both appearing first in 1576. One, by Humphrey Kerton—*The Mirror of Mans Lyfe*—went through at least five editions in the next ten years. The other, by George Gascoigne—"The View of Worldly Vanities"—comprised the first part of *The Droome of Doomes Day;*[9] Gascoigne claimed that his translation was made from an anonymous pamphlet, but this is not known to exist. In addition, a poetic synopsis of the *De miseria* by Stephen Gosson was printed at the end of the second edition of *The Mirror of Mans Lyfe* (1576).

In all countries, people read the work. It seems likely that Dante knew it.[10] Gianozzo Manetti, in his *De dignitate et excellentia hominis* (1532), systematically answered Innocent's arguments; and Bartolomeo Fazio, in *De excellentia et praestantia hominis* (1611) claimed to be writing the work Innocent had promised in his introduction—a task which Petrarch had once been asked to perform.[11] Erasmus probably knew it, for he wrote a similar work in his youth. It could be shown, I think, to have influenced Montaigne and Rabelais. Spanish and German Jesuits named it as reading for novices and as table reading in communities; its title appears in the *Directory of the Spiritual Exercises* as late as 1591.[12]

It is therefore important not merely as a reflection of late medieval thought, but as an influence upon those writers we regard as the first moderns. Why a work of such unmitigated gloom had so great a hold upon the reading public is a complicated question. It will not do merely to say that the Middle Ages was an age of faith in which renunciation of worldly things was

9 *STC* No. 11641. See *The Complete Works of George Gascoigne*, ed. John W. Cunliffe (2 vols.; Cambridge, Eng.: University Press, 1910), II, 209–274. Both translations are taken from the corrupt version discussed by Maccarrone, pp. xxiv–xxxii.

10 See Karl Vossler, *Mediaeval Culture* (New York: Ungar, 1929), II, 80, 117.

11 See Charles E. Trinkaus, Jr., *Adversity's Noblemen: The Italian Humanists on Happiness* (New York: Columbia University Press, 1940), pp. 20–21, 68–76, and Ernest Hatch Wilkins, *Life of Petrarch* (Chicago: University of Chicago Press, 1961), p. 140.

12 *Bibliotheca Instituti Historici Societatis Jesu* (Rome, 1955), VII, 294, 327; XI, 280, 297.

taken seriously. So were the earlier centuries of the Middle Ages;
but writings of this kind do not become prevalent in Europe until
late in the eleventh century. There are, to be sure, similar works
in earlier times, and it is possible to trace such ideas to the early
Fathers or indeed the Greeks. We shall not know for certain how
much the earlier Middle Ages was given to utterances about
contempt of the world until we have the completed studies of
Robert Bultot, which will trace the idea from the time of St.
Ambrose to Pope Innocent III.[13] But I think if we took earlier
works on the subject and put them beside works of the twelfth
and thirteenth centuries, we would find an important difference.
Just as a man of the eighteenth century would have found
such works monkish and outmoded, a little silly in their rhetoric
and altogether too unworldly for an enlightened age, a man of
the tenth century, say, would have found their tone and style
curiously violent and expostulary; they would have seemed un-
duly harsh and despairing, as if their authors were overstating
a one-sided case.

Yet these works appear at the end of the eleventh century and
in the twelfth century, just during that period of "renaissance"
when Europe seems to come alive. During this age we witness
the crusades, the building of cathedrals, a rise in heresies, the
growth of trade routes and towns, the origin of courtly love, the
struggle between church and state, the revival of jurisprudence,
the rise of the universities, new emphases in philosophy, science,
history, and poetry. Surely it is an age of increased secular spirit;
and such writings as Pope Innocent's treatise may represent a
"backlash" of religious sentiment, a warning which all must have
felt against these worldly activities. Was there not even a certain
pleasure in such sentiments, something more than the pleasure
of the safety-valve—a tragic, purgative emotion? Such, at any
rate, was the explanation of Willard Farnham:

[13] Robert Bultot, *Christianisme et valeurs humaines: La doctrine du
mépris du monde, en Occident, de S. Ambroise à Innocent III,* Tome IV, vols.
1 and 2 (Louvain and Paris: Nauwelaerts, 1963–   ); as announced, Dr.
Bultot's study will conclude with a treatment of the theme in medieval
French literature, and will continue with another work on the dignity of
man in the Middle Ages and the Renaissance.

Contempt of the World was for a time closely bound up with ascetic religious practice, but in the growing secularity of its appeal we have something which must be considered even as the paradoxical appeal of tragedy is considered. It began to be not only an ascetic duty to scorn the world, but also a pleasure, a truly artistic pleasure, a kind of tragic pleasure. It was emotional balance. Indeed it seems in the mysterious tragic fashion to have purged the complex emotions of the Renaissance and both to have expressed and to have calmed the uneasiness of an age which was impulsively shifting its realm of values from Heaven to earth.[14]

However, the twelfth-century renaissance was not just a burst of secular interest but a burst of energy in all directions, and this extended itself to an increased ascetic and reforming zeal. Churchmen became zealous in reforming clerical corruptions: such reformers as St. Peter Damian cried out against abuses in the Church, naively expecting monk-like virtues in lay leaders. They were of course disappointed. As a part of this trend, the monasteries now took a new position in society: reformed orders like the Cistercian became a retreat for churchly zealots. Early treatises on contempt of the world were written in monasteries by reformers like St. Anselm of Canterbury, Bernard of Morval, and St. Bernard of Clairvaux; one interpretation of these early works is that they reflect the disappointment of such figures in their hope that the Church should stand above the temporal order. The reformers retired in disillusionment and, from their cloisters, angrily denounced worldly pursuits.[15] In part, then, these works express the claims of church reformers against the temporal order.

14 Willard Farnham, *The Medieval Heritage of Elizabethan Tragedy* (Berkeley: University of California Press, 1936; reprinted, Oxford: Blackwell, 1956), p. 40.

15 See Gerhart B. Ladner, "Aspects of Medieval Thought on Church and State," *Review of Politics,* IX (1947), 403–422, and "The Concepts of 'Ecclesia' and 'Christianitas' and their Relation to the Idea of Papal 'Plenitudo Potestatis' from Gregory VII to Boniface VIII," *Miscellanea Historiae Pontificiae,* XVIII (1953), 49–77; Norman F. Cantor, "The Crisis of Western Monasticism, 1050–1130," *The American Historical Review,* LXVI (1960), 47–67.

There is a further explanation for these writings, which I do not find inconsistent with the two already advanced. Pope Innocent tells us in his introduction that he will in a future treatise "describe also the dignity of human nature; so that, as in the present work the proud man is brought low, in that the humble man will be exalted." So far as we know he never wrote it. It was a less intriguing subject. But his intention shows he recognized that "contempt of the world" and "dignity of man" were complementary, not contradictory. There had been a time when such works *did* raise both sides of the question. Both St. Anselm of Canterbury and Hugh of St. Victor allowed that there is something of Grace in created nature; both even agreed that there is some good in marriage. All of them could read in the Fathers, especially in St. Augustine, that in spite of our corruption we are good by nature, being the creatures of a good God and made in His image. Thus in everything Innocent says it is implicit that, as God's humble creatures, we do have dignity; but the expression of these two views is split up and the other side saved for another treatise. This tendency to split a two-edged subject was probably encouraged by "dialectic"—the art of disputation, favored at medieval universities—in which Innocent was well schooled; he had also legal training, and indeed often sounds like a lawyer arguing a case. Thus he acknowledges that he is making a one-sided statement. In this exaggeration of one viewpoint he and others were no doubt expressing an uneasiness they felt over an increasing worldliness, and showing their ambivalence about the worth of mundane things. They chose the side that seemed more important, more necessary. In stressing only that side, they unwittingly invited statements for the other; but such statements were not to come until the fourteenth century.

This polarization of an established idea is a curious event in intellectual history, and it is probably significant that it occurred during those years when dualistic heresies became a real threat to the Church. The influence of strict Catharist dualism—as opposed to the modified dualism of the earlier Bogomils—began in the 1140's; the sect was anathematized by the Third Lateran

Council in 1179.[16] In large part the great events of Innocent
III's papacy reflect the Church's struggle against Catharism. The
Dominican order and to an extent the Franciscan were founded
in hopes that they could turn the tide of dualism by preaching
and by love; the crusade against it, begun in 1209, attempted to
do so by military force, supplemented by the Inquisition. The
Fourth Lateran Council (1215), called to establish definitions
of orthodoxy, was chiefly prompted by the new heresy. In short,
Catharism made reforms in the world and the Church a far
more pressing concern.

But what was this threat? Surely not the extreme asceticism
of the Cathar *perfecti,* the monk-like initiates who renounced
the world and led lives of the utmost purity. That alone would
have occasioned little revulsion in the Church. Nor could it
have been the alleged sexual laxity of the *credentes* (adherents
who were not *perfecti*) ; for this, if indeed it existed, was a side-
effect and by no means part of the Cathar doctrine. It seems as
unlikely that the extreme spirituality of the sect would by itself
have caused alarm. Rather it was the pessimistic side of their
doctrine, their conviction that matter is evil and the soul a
prisoner in an evil body, which offended orthodoxy. Such a belief led them to deny those Christian dogmas which involved
world and flesh—the Incarnation, the sacrament of the mass,
the virgin birth—and led them even to repudiate procreation:
they thought birth itself an evil, since it imprisoned the soul
in matter. Whereas the Church taught that the biblical com-
mand to wax and multiply was the justification, however weak,
for sexuality, and that marriage was therefore among the grades
of perfection, the extraordinary otherworldliness of the Cathars

16 On Catharism see Steven Runciman, *The Medieval Manichee: A Study
of the Christian Dualist Heresy* (Cambridge, Eng.: University Press, 1960),
pp. 116–170; Jeffrey Burton Russell, *Dissent and Reform in the Early Middle
Ages* (Berkeley and Los Angeles: University of California Press, 1965), pp.
188–229; René Nelli, *Le phénomène Cathare: Perspectives philosophiques,
morales, et iconographiques* (Toulouse, 1964); Daniel Walther, "A Survey
of Recent Research on the Albigensian Cathari," *Church History,* XXXIV
(1965), 146–177.

swept all this to one side: the race, they believed, should let itself become extinct. Catharism thus challenged the ingrained belief of Augustinian Christianity that the creatures of the physical universe, however "mutable" and corrupted, are good, and that evil, being parasitic, is "nothing."

Writings on contempt of the world, already a traditional expression of the reforming spirit, were available to Innocent and others as a weapon against the dualist heresy. Such works set forth a Christian dualism which equated evil with human error, not with matter: they condemned abuses, not earthly existence itself; they pointed to the misery, the transitoriness and vanity of the human condition, not to abstract evil as a principle inherent in the physical universe; and their purpose was to improve the kind of lives men lead, not to make earthly life extinct. No doubt Innocent had this more moderate position in mind while writing the *De miseria*. Still, it is hard to understand why he emphasized only the pessimistic side of Christian dualism. St. Francis and Alain de Lille both dwelt upon the goodness and rightness of creation, and it would have been as effective a choice for Innocent to single out, as he promised to do, the dignity of human nature. Pessimism was, it appears, deeply inherent in the thought and feeling of the late twelfth century, and the *De miseria* shares in this predilection for gloom. Perhaps both Catharism and orthodoxy were reacting against the new secular spirit of the twelfth century. Or perhaps they were merely reacting against each other. At all events, the Cathars in their pessimism went very far—as far as the *endura,* ritual suicide by starvation; orthodox writers like Innocent were satisfied to inculcate *contemptus mundi* as a frame of mind.

II · THE AUTHOR

It would at any rate be a mistake to interpret the *De miseria* solely as a personal utterance. It was a traditional kind of writing for which its age had conceived a taste. Innocent's work is the classic of the genre, but this is not because he brought to it an unusual personal zeal or inspiration. Rather he brought to it an education in theology, rhetoric, and canon law: it is a learned work—learned in its content, learned in its polished style. It is not a mere scholastic exercise written to while away the time, but an encyclopedic treatment of a favorite topic; and no work of its kind was ever to surpass it.

That he wrote it when he did, however, may suggest a tinge of personal motive. Innocent was born in 1160 or 1161; his given name was Lothario. He belonged to a powerful Roman family, the Segni (which called themselves Conti). He was bred to a career of statesmanship, studied at the universities of Paris and Bologna, and by the age of 30 was already well experienced in ecclesiastical politics. He had been ordained a deacon, and was not ordained priest until after his election to the papacy. His uncle, Pope Clement III, made him a cardinal in 1190; but in 1191 Celestine III ascended the papal throne and, being a member of the Orsini family (rivals of the Conti), relieved the young cardinal of his duties. During these years of unemployment (1191–1198) Lothario wrote several learned works, among them the *De miseria,* probably in 1195. Because of this circumstance, historians often regard it as the work of an idle hand. Professor Packard, for instance, remarks, "We are obliged to agree with Luchaire, the learned French biographer of Innocent III, that the treatise is merely a scholar's exercise, a display of technique. It reveals his abilities, not his opinions."[17] Perhaps so. But why did he choose this, rather than another subject? Why, for example, had he not written the treatise on man's dignity instead? During these years of idleness, with a rival family in power, he had a motive other than boredom or ambition: to remind himself of the vanity of earthly pursuits.

It must not be thought that I am proposing a "sour-grapes" interpretation. Rather, I believe it seemed fitting to write about the misery of the human condition and the vanity of earthly pursuits precisely to remove bitterness or disappointment from his heart and adopt the proper attitude of contempt toward worldly things. So, at least, he described his motive in his prologue—to

---

17 Sidney R. Packard, *Europe and the Church under Innocent III* (New York: H. Holt and Co., 1927), p. 13.

"put down pride." "Fitting" and "proper" suggest, as I mean
them to, a ritual or traditional quality in his actions; but this
ritual quality does not make such actions the less sincere. Our
modern suspicion of ritual, our habit of being "relaxed" when
performing ceremonious actions, is likely to do us a disservice
here; for ritual acts are not "hollow" unless we make them so.
We know we are expected to congratulate a bridegroom or a
prize-winner; but only cynics would say that such sentiments,
being traditional, are therefore unfelt. If they conceal self-pity
or envy they likely conceal it as much from the speaker as from
the recipient. So with the young cardinal's motives: he wrote of
an attitude appropriate to his circumstances. A similar personal
motive can perhaps be found in the other two treatises he wrote
during the same years—*The Sacred Mystery of the Altar* and
The Four Kinds of Marriage. Both are, like the *De miseria,*
tours de force; they show a great expertise in mystical symbolism
or allegory. There is no doubt that they bore witness to his learning and rhetorical skill. Luchaire, speaking of the cardinals who
elected him Pope, remarks, "One must believe, because they
said so, that the prestige of Lothario dei Segni as theologian,
moralist, and writer was not unimportant to his accession."[18] But
this does not mean he wrote them out of ambition. His circumstances drew him to these subjects. One work deals with the
"sacred mystery of the altar," which only a priest can perform;
and at this time he was not yet a priest—he was to be ordained
after his election to the papacy. The other is about the kinds of
marriage (between man and woman, between Christ and the
Church, between God and the just soul, between the Word and
human nature); and when elected, Innocent was said to have
had a vision that he would "marry his mother," that is, the
Church. The treatises suggest that he had been thinking about
this possible priesthood and this mystical marriage all along.

In his behavior on being elected Pope (January 8, 1198),
there is a similar kind of ritualized or conventional behavior.
The election was held on the same day the old Pope died. There
were many candidates; Celestine himself had attempted to name

[18] Achille Luchaire, *Innocent III,* I (Paris: Librairie Hachette, 1907), 12.

his successor. But Lothario, though the youngest member of the curia (he was then thirty-seven) was elected. At first he refused the honor; he "wept and sobbed" before giving in. Popes- and bishops-elect had behaved thus from early times; tears and protests upon election were conventional acts of humility. That he behaved thus at all may be a conventional pious legend (one notes that three white doves are said to have flown into the room and settled at his right side); but very likely such conventional legends affected men's behavior on such occasions, more at least than they affected that of doves. These conventions are all very medieval, of course, but we shall misunderstand the age gravely if we suppose that they were sham. They represent traditional attitudes and postures of the kind one finds in any small, closed group. Such traditions of suitable behavior are still deeply entrenched in ecclesiastical circles—one has but to read *L'osservatore romano* for a notion of them. One might compare the ritual of "drafting" political candidates in modern elections. Thus on the day after his election Innocent wrote: "Many would have been . . . worthier than we of such an honor. Convinced of our inability, we at first refused this office, too heavy for our weak shoulders, but had to give in to the insistence of our brothers. In prolonging resistance we could have opened the door to a dangerous schism, or seemed to oppose the decrees of the divine will."[19]

During the years of his papacy (he died in 1216) Pope Innocent III wielded great power, and claimed that power for himself with confidence. This is, of course, what makes modern readers suspect his motives in writing the *De miseria*. Had he retreated to a monastery, no one would raise the point. Had he become a cynical or debauched pope in love with temporal power, there would be some justice in it. But he was not of this kind. Historians have disagreed about the nature of his claims to power, some insisting that he ruled veritably as an emperor over Italy and all Europe. It is certainly true that he held power—he was able to wield the weapons of medieval popes, excommunication and the interdict, as far away as England and Norway. On the

[19] *Ibid.*, I, 25.

other hand, he insisted that he was concerned not with feudal matters but with spiritual ones—with sin or heresy. Only in Italy, where he was a temporal lord in his own right, could he be said to have exercised direct temporal power. That he *had* power we cannot deny; and in the next century his writings were used to *claim* temporal power for the papacy. We cannot deny that he wielded what power he had and that he believed in his right to do so. But he was committed to Church reform. The power of a reformed Church over the temporal order could scarcely have seemed other than a good thing, for the temporal order was corrupt and temporal rulers were not "vicars of Christ."

This commitment to the reform of Church and "world" helps to solve the great riddle about the *De miseria*—how the same man could write a treatise so harshly ascetical and then rise to such heights of political power in the Church. The reformers' zeal indeed demanded political power for a reformed and reforming Church. And the world's corruption was exactly what made it subject to ecclesiastical power—in the *De miseria* Innocent says much less of the Church's inadequacies than of the world's. His contention that the temporal order is transitory, vain, and corrupt does not therefore contradict his belief in papal authority and church power, but supports it. There was, that is, a traditional relationship between the idea of reform and "contempt of the world."

III · WRITINGS ON CONTEMPT OF THE WORLD

Innocent called his work *De miseria humane conditionis*. It has been popularly called *De contemptu mundi,* but "contempt of the world" was a tag for this *kind* of writing and was attached to his work by scribes.[20] In speaking of "contempt of the world," we are not referring to any ubiquitous and existential gloom, but to a specific and historical complex of ideas, expressed in a set language. The writings which propound these ideas, as we have

[20] Maccarrone, pp. xxxii–xxxv.

seen, appear in Europe in the twelfth century and disappear in the seventeenth. There are some 300 prose works which are examples of the genre, and about 150 or 200 poems; perhaps half of these are unpublished. One would suppose that such treatises could be found among the Fathers from earliest Christian times; certainly particular sentiments are ubiquitous and can readily be traced to ancient philosophers and the Old Testament. The phrase itself, "contempt of the world," is as old at least as St. Jerome, and perhaps has its origins in the stoic idea of indifference to material things and to pleasure or pain. Something *like* a "De contemptu mundi" may be found in such works as St. Cyprian's treatise on the plague *(De mortalitate)* or in St. Ambrose's *De bono mortis,* yet these earlier works simply do not sound like the later ones—they do not use the same language or touch upon the same topics.

Works on contempt of the world generally deal with quite standard subjects, and it will perhaps be easiest to summarize these. For the treatises are very repetitious. They quickly became vehicles for rhetorical flights, and their variations are rather in literary devices than in ideas. Their chief themes or *topoi* are the following:

1. *The corruption of the natural order,* and in particular that of the human body. Many treatises *de contemptu mundi* give morbid descriptions of man's physical being, diseases and pain, and the terrors of birth and death.

2. *The mutability of earthly things,* the argument that worldly things are unsatisfying because they are temporary. The principle of Fortune's wheel was often used to illustrate this fact, as was the *ubi sunt* motif (the traditional question, "Where is Alexander?" "Where is Caesar?" "Where are the snows of yesteryear?" etc.) . One finds diatribes against the fickleness of women, certainly a form of mutability, and protracted descriptions of old age.

3. *The vanity of earthly things,* the argument that earthly pursuits are *per se* dissatisfying even before time or Fortune has removed their objects. Thus for example one's ambitions for money or power give rise to sleeplessness, fear, and worry. The

phrase of I John 2:16, that everything in the world is "the lust of the flesh, the lust of the eyes, and the pride of life" furnished a convenient way of categorizing these earthly vanities.

4. *The evils of the social order.* The three estates (Nobles, Clergy, Commons), and the various professions in each, were scrutinized and condemned·for their corruption and wrongdoing. It was remarked that judges took bribes, lawyers defended the unjust if rich and let the just die if poor, doctors treated only for money, and so on. Monastic and ecclesiastical abuses were condemned, kings and popes chastised. Ostensibly these evils of the social order illustrate how the world deserves to be despised; yet the implication was that particular abuses should be reformed, so that in some degree the works have a satiric function.

5. *Punishment or reward in the afterlife.* Some treatises include elaborate descriptions of heaven and hell, which suggest by contrast the insignificance of earthly life and the important consequences of scorning or espousing the world.

The earliest work which has any marked similarity to the host of later writings *de contemptu mundi* is the *Apologeticum de contemptu mundi* of St. Peter Damian, written in the third quarter of the eleventh century. It is a complaint against laxness in monastic discipline, and takes part in the climate of monastic reform characteristic of that age. The Cluniac reforms of the early tenth century had paved the way for other reforms in the centuries that followed. The Carthusian and Cistercian orders were to be founded in the late eleventh century. Early in the eleventh century celibacy of the Latin clergy was declared obligatory, and later in that century Pope Gregory VII, while increasing papal power, enforced reforms vigorously. To this reform of monasteries, and of the Church generally, St. Peter Damian devoted his life. In the *Apologeticum* he arranged his points according to the three monastic vows—poverty, obedience, and chastity. He castigates monks for their interest in money, their tendency to leave the seclusion of the monastery, and their fondness for rich garments and other vanities. He blames their anger, drunkenness, loss of fervor, hypocrisy, and lechery. But he then turns his attention to offenses outside the monastery among society in general: illicit and incestuous marriages, the selling of justice, avarice. He ends his work by warning sinners against the horrors of the tomb and the snares of worldly life: "And so you will see how quickly this short life will pass away. You will see how the world declares with clear indications its coming end. . . . Wherefore as the apples of a hollow tree brought forth too soon fall before they are ripe, so shall men in their bitter exile die before coming to the fullness of age."[21]

In the next generation, St. Anselm of Canterbury wrote similar works. One of the great original theologians of his age, he served as Archbishop of Canterbury under the king, William Rufus, and is known for his struggle with Rufus and Henry over lay investiture and homage from clerics for their benefices. In a short prose work called "Exhortation to Scorn Temporal Things and Desire Things Eternal,"[22] he addresses himself to monks, using essentially the same arguments we have seen in St. Peter Damian. He exhorts his hearers to have continence in speech, appearance, food, dress, thought, and laughter; to pray, to be penitent, and to despise worldly things. He mentions the traditional three sins of I John 2:16—avarice, gluttony, and vainglory. He castigates monks for pride, boasting, ostentation, the love of prosperity, and popular glory. Chiefly he would have men be humble and patient in prosperity or adversity, avoiding wrath, envy, indignation, hatred, or detraction, and scorning worldly joys in order to gain eternal ones.

Sometimes attributed to him is a poem *de contemptu mundi*,[23] although it is probably by his contemporary and confrere, Roger of Bec (d. 1090). Approximately 900 lines long, it is written in unrhymed elegiac couplets. Intended as a warning against espousal of worldly things, it draws upon numerous medieval themes, lashing out satirically in many directions. While addressed chiefly to monks, it extends its warnings to all Christians. It is apparently the first serious attempt to treat contempt of the world in poetry. It states as its theme "what befits a monk

21 J. P. Migne, ed., *Patrologia Latina* (221 vols.; Paris, 1844–1903 [hereafter abbreviated PL], 145: 289.

22 *PL* 158: 677–686.

23 *PL* 158: 687–706.

and what sort of person he should be." He marshalls the sins he blames under the traditional three divisions—the lust of the eyes, the lust of the flesh, and pride of life—as Innocent does in his second book. Thus he chastises the love of various kinds of possessions, denigrates the human body for its weakness and lust, and warns against honors and power. Dispersed through the work are passages on the horrors of old age, the temptations which women put in men's way, the falls of great men, and the passing away of the pagan philosophers. The poem ends with a summation of the brevity of human life and its miseries, together with a reminder that man is created in God's image, that virtue and the love of God should be his study, and that heavenly bliss will be his reward.

A similar work, by Hugh of St. Victor, "On the Vanity of the World and the Use of Transitory Things," is in the form of a dialogue.[24] It names five principal vanities of earthly life: human endeavors in general, riches, property, marriage, and intellectual activity. There is a long passage on the brevity and mutability of life. It employs the *ubi sunt* theme, and compares those who love this world to shipwrecked men cast into the sea. And of course it counsels men to prefer the "works of restoration" in nature, law, and grace to the works of their fallen and corrupted condition.

Along with these writings of the late eleventh and early twelfth centuries, we find a group of anonymous treatises and lyric poems which can for the most part be traced to Cistercian and Cluniac monasteries.[25] About 1140, at Cluny, a monk named Bernard—sometimes called Bernard of Morval—wrote a long poem called *De contemptu mundi*[26] in bombastic leonine hexameters; but in spite of its heavy-handedness, it is a remarkable achievement. It is a bitter satire which attacks every conceivable

[24] *PL* 176: 703–740.

[25] Among these is the important work, *Speculum peccatoris, PL* 40: 983–992. See also B. Hauréau, *Des poèmes latins attribués à S. Bernard* (Paris, 1890), especially pp. i–v.

[26] Bernard of Morval, *De contemptu mundi: A Bitter Satirical Poem of 3000 lines upon the Morals of the XIIth Century,* ed. A. C. Hoskier (London, Bernard Quaritch, Ltd., 1929).

abuse, and ends with a description of heaven and hell probably known to Dante.

The influence of these earlier works, especially Hugh of St. Victor's, may be seen in the "Pious Meditations on the Knowledge of Human Life,"[27] attributed to St. Bernard of Clairvaux. This treatise, more than any other, influenced Innocent's work. The author begins with a discussion of man's dignity. Man, made in the image of God, is capable of knowing God and having access to him, so that the rational mind is the image of God and ought to control the choices of will. Prayer is the means by which the mind grasps principles of conduct and follows the love of God; when it falls from this it becomes lost in vanity, curiosity, cupidity, pleasure, lechery, envy, wrath, and despair. The alternative is confession, repentance, and continued virtue; and the basis of virtue is the love of God, contempt for worldly things, and awareness of death and judgment. The prime requisite of repentance, however, is self-knowledge; and to this end the author undertakes a treatment of man's nature from his birth, his conduct in life, and his manner of death. The schema is the one Pope Innocent III uses—the *ingressus, progressus,* and *egressus.* A passage from St. Bernard's treatment of the *ingressus* will show its similarity to Innocent's treatise:

> Sinners in their sin give birth to a sinner and nurse him on sin. The wretched bring forth the wretched into this misery of light. And one gets nothing from them but misery and sin and this corruptible body. I hasten, then, to them that have gone hence at the body's death. When I look upon their tombs I find nothing in them but ashes and the vile worm and horror. What I am, they were; and what they are, I am to be. And what am I? man, made of liquid humor. In the moment of conception, I was conceived of human semen; and then that coagulated foam, by growing a little, was made flesh. After that, weeping and wailing I was given into the exile of this world; and, lo, now I am dying full of iniquities and abominations. And finally I am put before the stern Judge to render account of my works. . . . Hear, o man, what you were before birth, what you are from birth to death, and what you will be after

27 *PL* 184: 485–508.

this life. Truly there was a time when you were not; then you were made of vile matter and rolled about in the vilest rag, you were nursed in your mother's womb on menstrual blood, and your tunic was your outer skin. . . . Nothing else is man but nasty sperm, a sack of dung, food for worms. . . . Why, then, art thou proud, o dust and ashes, conceived in guilt, born to misery, living in punishment, dying in anguish?[28]

In the centuries which followed, contempt of the world became a set theme for rhetorical flights. Treatises on the subject were written by many figures of the fourteenth and fifteenth centuries in all parts of Europe. One should at least mention that the first book of *The Imitation of Christ* fits the *de contemptu* genre, and that Erasmus, in his youth, wrote a wholly traditional work on the subject. Moreover, there are a dozen or more treatises on the subject by Italian humanists. Works by Poggio Bracciolini, Giovanni Conversino, and Coluccio Salutati very clearly belong to the tradition, as does Petrarch's *Secretum*. For the most part these Renaissance works use traditional terminology and traditional arguments. Several, like that of Maffeo Veggio, are in dialogue form and present both sides of the argument. In a dialogue by Celso Maffei the speakers never come to any conclusion or compromise but end by agreeing to dine together, which of course deals a blow to contempt of the world. Everyone will remember the unresolved character of Petrarch's *Secretum,* in which St. Augustine argues for contempt of worldly vanities while the poet himself ruminates upon love, learning, and fame. Petrarch used all the traditional fodder of the *De contemptu mundi,* but his great intellect saw and expressed the contrarieties of his age more candidly and inclusively than anyone else had done. By adopting the dialogue form Petrarch broke with the tradition of Pope Innocent III—that of cutting to one side the possible case for the opposition—and presented to his readers what the age presented to him, a dilemma. He further broke with tradition by adopting in place of the usual oracular and invective tone a meditative and personal one. Certainly it is endearing that while previous writers had urged others to

28 *PL* 184: 487, 490.

scorn the world, Petrarch had simply and honestly discussed whether he himself could and should do so, and had concluded that he could and should, but might not.

While some humanists were writing on contempt of the world, however, others were writing about the dignity of man. Gianozzo Manetti, in his *De dignitate et excellentia hominis* (1532), purported to be writing the treatise which Pope Innocent III had promised, and Bartolomeo Fazio in 1611 attempted to refute Pope Innocent point by point. These Renaissance treatises are humanistic, but in general their premises are Christian, and Professor Trinkaus has shown that some writers on human dignity turned to the theology of St. Augustine for support.[29] I should, however, like to point to an important fact about the *number* of such treatises. Given the usual notion of the Renaissance, one would expect to find a tradition of writings on the dignity of man growing up in Italy during the fourteenth century and in France and England in the fifteenth and sixteenth centuries. And one would expect to find treatises on contempt of the world waning and disappearing during this period. But there is only a handful of treatises on the dignity of man beyond the twenty or so which Professor Trinkaus has dealt with; none are earlier than the late fourteenth century; and none seems to have been written outside Italy. I do not mean to suggest that the *idea* of human dignity did not occur in other nations; but the treatises on human dignity were a brief fashion in Italy during the Renaissance, whereas the treatises on contempt of the world were a long-standing tradition in all nations which did not waver until the *end* of the Renaissance.

For all their zeal and harshness, works on contempt of the world conceal a fundamental strain of worldliness. At first glance they look like medievalism itself, but everywhere implicit is a feeling of some limited worth in mundane things. The writers are avowedly concerned with the world. Their descriptions of the misery of life and the mutability of earthly joys imply that earthly pleasure is good. Their argument that all worldly pursuits are disappointing suggests the premise that disappointing

29 Trinkaus, pp. 21–22, 92–93.

things are to be eschewed just because they fail to please; and
indeed such works often name the alternative to life's discomforts not as a heavenly reward but as an earthly one—peace of
mind. The satiric aspect of these writings, moreover, posits the
desirability of moral and social corrections in the here and now.
Lastly, their tendency to rhetorical flourish suggests that their
authors were, in Dr. Johnson's phrase, able "to receive some
solace of the miseries of life, from consciousness of the delicacy
with which they felt, and the eloquence with which they be-
wailed them."

Perhaps it will be easiest to pinpoint the ultimate meaning-
fulness of this tradition, at least for English literature, if we can
look at the very last literary work in which it makes a recog-
nizable appearance, and ask what is different or changed in it.
It seems to me that the last work which shows significant traces
of the tradition is *Gulliver's Travels*. I hope this will not seem
like thesis-mongering; Swift was, after all, an Anglican divine,
by nature old-fashioned and pessimistic. Works on the misery of
the human condition were current in England during the seventeenth century, and as Louis Landa has shown, Swift must have
read some of them.[30] Indeed in his sermon on the Poor Man's
Contentment, Swift actually talked about "the miserable condition of man during the whole progress of his life"—a phrase
which echoes Pope Innocent III. In *Gulliver's Travels* he deals
with most of the traditional subject matter of *de contemptu*
treatises. In the voyage to Laputa, he criticizes vain learning—
the sin of curiosity in Christian writings. In the voyage to Glubb-
dubdrib he shows that fame is untrustworthy as a reward for
human endeavor. In the passage about the Struldbrugs he deals
with the horrors of old age. His attention to the vileness of the
human body, often chalked up to psychopathology, was wholly
in line with *de contemptu* tradition. In Gulliver's discourse to
the King of the Houyhnhnms, we find criticism of doctors and
lawyers, the unequal distribution of wealth, gluttony, avarice,
political ambition, corruption in government, and the irresponsi-
bility of nobles. In the description of the Yahoos we find such

---

[30] *Gulliver's Travels and Other Writings,* ed. Louis A. Landa (Boston:
Houghton Mifflin, 1960), pp. xxi–xxv.

traditional *de contemptu* topics as the condemnation of avarice, unnatural appetites, and the vanity and lechery of women. In short, Swift touches upon all the conventional themes of corrupt nature, the transitoriness and vanity of earthly pursuits, and the ills of the social order—all but the expectation of a life hereafter, of which he says nothing. As for human dignity, he believes in it as a possibility rather than a reality, and in this respect he is in some ways closer to the Middle Ages than to the Enlightenment. Yet of course his emphasis falls upon the necessity, not of renouncing and scorning the world, but of improving it. Even here he was anticipated by earlier writers *de contemptu mundi* and like them he might have had little hope that men would follow his counsels; yet no earlier writer on contempt of the world would have centered his work so exclusively in the realm of human affairs, none would so much have neglected the afterlife, and none would have put so much emphasis on man's capacity for reason. The difference is not one of content or of kind, but one of emphasis and degree—and one of style.

IV · THE STYLE OF THE "DE MISERIA"

Although style and content cannot be completely divorced, the content of the *De miseria* creates few difficulties. The work is organized in the clearest way; most of its ideas are not unfamiliar to us; and its pessimism and hopelessness should give no trouble to readers of Kierkegaard and Sartre, or of modern novels. Some of its organizational motifs, which would have seemed quite natural to the medieval reader, will be unfamiliar, and these I have mentioned in the footnotes. The plan of the three books, "ingress, progress, and egress," had, as we have seen, been used before. Book Two is divided according to a traditional division of sins or temptations—"the lust of the flesh, the lust of the eyes, and pride of life" or "pleasures, riches, and honors."[31] Book Three is really a treatise on the Last Things (death, judgment,

---

[31] The division is based on I John 2:15–16; see Donald R. Howard, *The Three Temptations* (Princeton, N. J.: Princeton University Press, 1966), pp. 43–75, for a history of the idea.

Hell, and Heaven), with Heaven omitted. In Books I (11-16) and II there is implicit a reference to the three estates—"nobles, clergy, and commons." But these matters should give no trouble; once aware of them we will find the book easier. What *will* create difficulties for the modern reader is the book's manner and style. Here, of course, the translator must cross a Rubicon of outmoded rhetorical conventions, and the reader must do what he can to feel at home in new terrain.

In revising Miss Dietz's translation, which aimed at literal accuracy, I have sometimes resorted to paraphrase. I have tried to retain any notable characteristics of the original style which are not, to us, downright outlandish; but as best I could I have turned medieval "eloquence," when it seems absurd in present-day English, into some modern equivalent. The last sentence of the work is a good example. In the original, the long list of synonyms is a list of pairs—"fear and trembling, toil and trouble," and so on; it is a tour de force of word-choice, its effect relying in part upon rhymes, alliteration, and assonance. In modern English the rhythm of some seventeen pairs of adjectives is merely tedious, so I rearranged them into groups having a rhythm more suitable to modern ears. But I tried to approximate the prosody of the original: it seems like effective bombast still, and it is an essential of the original style. I hope the resulting sentence has somewhat the effect upon the reader which the author intended it to have. No translator ever fully captures the style of his work, and the best one can do is follow one's instincts and select what seems most effective, adjudicating between literal sense and stylistic effect, and between medieval notions or tastes and modern ones.

Part of the difficulty is that the original has *two* styles. One is the ancient rhetoric of the Fathers, shaped by patristic authorities and of course the Bible, and formulated in various texts of rhetoric. This style is balanced and eloquent, having the weight of tradition to give it dignity; it reflects daily study of the Bible as the source of revealed truth. For example,

> No man should trust that he is free of punishment who knows
> he is free of guilt. He who stands should see to it that he fall not.
> For often the innocent man is condemned and the guilty man set

free; the pious man is punished, the impious honored; Jesus is crucified, Barabbas set free. And indeed, these days the quiet man is thought useless, the religious man is thought a hypocrite, and the simple man is thought a fool. (I, 30)

On the other hand, the author turns sometimes to the *logical* examination of his subject, as for example in his treatment of hell's punishments. Here the style is crisply scholastic and scientific; it is grounded in logic, and in the systematic citing of Scripture as authority for doctrinal points. For example,

> The wicked are enveloped not only in exterior but in interior darkness, because they lack spiritual as well as corporeal light. For it is written, "Away with the wicked lest he see the glory of God," who alone will be in "everlasting light."
>
> The wicked, however, will suffer such anguish in their punishments that they will scarcely be able to think of anything because of it. . . . (III, 10)

This equipment Innocent brought with him from his theological training at Paris and his legal training at Bologna. With these styles the author, as one critic phrases it, "discourses with the rhetorician's calm, and with the secure coldness of the scholar."[32] There is little sense of a profound, intense feeling; it would be wrong to suppose the work a personal description of a state of mind, or an expression of a deeply felt personal conviction. But it is *not* a mere scholastic exercise. Very likely we shall do best to view it as an oratorical work which presents a collection of propositions briefly argued; it is religious or biblical—indebted to the ancient tradition of wisdom literature—and at the same time logical and scientific. Hence it sounds at times piously rhetorical and at times coldly learned.[33]

Since the seventeenth century this kind of prose style, like the subject matter itself, has seemed foreign. Partly this is owing to changes in taste, for prose styles pass out of fashion like everything else. But the change goes deeper: it goes, indeed, to a

[32] Antonio Viscardi, *Saggio sulla letteratura religiosa del medio Evo romanzo* (R. Università di Padova, Pubb. della Facoltà di Lettere e Filosofia, III [1932]), 67.

[33] *Ibid.*, pp. 63–76.

revolution in our most fundamental principles of thought. We must therefore remind ourselves, while reading a work such as this, of the attitudes about writing its first audience would have had. These I believe can be reduced to three kinds of unconscious mental habits:

1. *An attitude toward words.* To us, more than to medieval men, words stand for things only by habit or tradition; we have not put word-magic behind us altogether, but when we try to define terms and use them in precise senses we are mindful that their meanings are arbitrary. To medieval men words had meaning chiefly because it was their nature; they were symbols, of course, but so might anything be a symbol—a lion, a rose, colors, numbers. The rose *itself* symbolized martyrdom because its color was that of blood, and the *words* "rose" and "blood" took their importance from the things they stood for. Symbolism was therefore very real to them. Similarities in the *sounds* of words seemed to them a sign of some hidden similarity or correspondence in the nature of things themselves. Medieval authors were always ready to catch such hints and to be awed by them. We shall mistake Innocent's spirit very gravely if we think he "liked word-play"—if we suppose, that is, that in his puns he was being cute, witty, or eccentric. For example, in the case of deformed children (I, 5) he reports that *homines* has to do with *abhominationes,* and that for these children "forte melius fuisset provisum si nunquam *prodiissent ad visum.*" Such a sentence would, I believe, have made the author seem very perspicacious indeed; it would have provoked wonder at the proportionableness of things and at his own exactitude. Thus he informs us that these deformed children "ut monstra monstrantur"—they are, that is, at once "monsters" and things to be "demonstrated" and gawked at.

This eager attention to the "real" meanings of words explains the medieval fondness for "etymologies."[34] Eve's name *means* misery: "For what is the name 'Eva,' when examined carefully,

---

[34] Ernst Robert Curtius, *European Literature and the Latin Middle Ages,* trans. Willard R. Trask (Bollingen Series XXXVI, New York: Harper & Bros., 1953), pp. 495–500. In his etymology of "Eva" Innocent advanced a new interpretation; it differs, at all events, from that of Isidore's *Etymologiae.*

but *Eu!* plus *Ah!*—these words being interjections of sorrow or great pain" (I, 6). The "real" meaning got through this etymology tells something about reality itself. It is not unlike the modern superstition of those who feel that *education* has to do with "leading forth" or that *grave* essentially means "heavy." In modern times, however, the love of etymologies concerns itself largely with the art of using words; in medieval times it concerned itself more with the essential meaning of things themselves. Hence all such attention to puns, double meanings, roots, and phonetic similarity serves as justification for a proposition. "Eva" means *eu* plus *ah;* and this *proves* that man was born to misery.

Metaphors, also, had great stature. They were not solely "figures of speech" to be admired for their art; they were correspondences which gave clues to the essential nature or meaning of things. Up to a point, they are still that for us, but we are more restrained. When Innocent compares man to a tree (I, 8), *we* may throw up our hands; but medieval readers would have been impressed. Because metaphors describe meaningful correspondences among things, a mixed metaphor did not betray bad thinking, as it does now. When Innocent says "For your eye is never so pure as to keep the brightness of the whole body; you add always some yeast that corrupts the whole" (II, 4), he is making *two* points—(1) that even when the eye sees clearly, the remainder of the body can still lead one to sin, and (2) that there is an inevitable tendency toward corruption in man (from original sin). Medieval writers did not have ideas of "organic" unity as we now do; two separate comparisons hint at two separate principles. They would not have seemed incompatible, and their "mixed" quality would have seemed not awkward but wondrous.

2. *An attitude toward books.* For us as for medieval men books contain facts, but in nothing like the same degree. The intelligent reader in modern times is trained to be skeptical about what he reads, and is much less predisposed to take the written word for granted; we are as likely to cite an author for his "interesting opinion" as for his factual authority. But in the Middle Ages it was otherwise. They were very reverent to the written word, and very credulous of what they read. An "author" was

an "authority"—that is, his book was an authority, especially if
old. The authority belonged to the written text, not the man;
and the more recent author had to be satisfied with the appel-
lation, *magister*. Nature itself, to the extent that it was considered a norm, was called a book.[35] Indeed the source of revealed truth, the Bible, was a collection of "authors" writing
under the inspiration of the Holy Ghost, so that God Himself
could be understood as an "author" and the Bible could be
called Truth.[36]

The scriptural citations in the *De miseria* have therefore a
function very different from what we are likely to imagine: they
are not illustrations for the sake of clarity, and not "interesting
opinions" for the sake of comparison. They are the truth. They
prove the statement to which they are attached. Medieval men
might have responded to them somewhat as we respond to footnotes or statistical tables—the difference being that they came
not, as footnotes or statistical tables do, from "other researchers,"
but from God. Quotations from the Fathers were not of course
inspired as the Bible was; but they had great authority, being
by Saints.

Quotations from classical authors have a different status, but
still a very high one. What Horace or Juvenal wrote was not,
like Scripture, inspired by the Holy Ghost. But it was written,
and it was old. What was written and old would have been considered true if interpreted rightly. Thus Innocent quotes Horace:
"You may drive nature out with a pitchfork but she will come
back again" (I, 17). Horace is actually referring to a farmer's
problem in getting rid of weeds; but Innocent makes it refer
to the problem of removing lustful habits. Pagan authors did
not know revealed truth, but their God-given intellect and
wisdom permitted them to say true things. Thus Vergil, it was
thought, had prophesied the birth of Christ in the fourth
Eclogue; the medieval reader, with Revelation on his side, could

35 *Ibid.*, 319–322.
36 So Innocent calls it, for example, in II, 5 and II, 13. On "authority"
see M.-D. Chenu, *La théologie au xii siècle* (Études de Philosophie Médiéval,
XLV, Paris, 1957), 351–365.

see this plainly, though Vergil could not. A quotation did not by any means have to be understood in context; it was true as a statement, whatever went before or after. Probably Innocent had his classical quotations from collections of sayings or from a work like the *Polycraticus* which quotes classical authors; perhaps he did not know the context. But if Horace was actually writing of a farmer's trouble with weeds, this did not matter—he had said the truth about lustful thoughts anyway.

The *exempla* are similarly used for authority. In modern times we give examples to illustrate or clarify a point. Occasionally, we use examples as "anecdotal evidence" to show that something has occurred at least once; but there is nothing empirical about medieval *exempla*. They are almost never drawn from the author's own observation, they are drawn from his reading. Thus Innocent tells us the anecdote of the woman who ate her children (I, 29). The grisly tale illustrates his point and gives it emotional appeal, but what is important is its power to validate what he has been saying; this comes not from the fact that "it really happened"; it comes from the fact that it is in Josephus' *De bello Judaico*.[37] That is, it gets its authority and importance from being in an old book.

3. *An attitude toward style*. Style was a set of rhetorical principles. The medieval author would have learned these from textbooks and from the example of "authorities." His aim, like ours, was clarity and elegance; but, as one would expect, he had different ideas about these qualities. To us clarity is gained by specific details, examples, transitions, or summaries; and because we are making clear "our own thoughts," style has for us a personal or individual quality. To the Middle Ages "one's own thoughts" were inconsequential—truth might be expressed differently by different writers, but it was still one truth and not relative to individual utterances or contexts. Style was therefore not an individual quality which reflected the writer's personality or philosophy; it was a tool and an ornament.

For the Middle Ages, man's understanding was clouded as a

[37] Maccarrone, p. xli, thinks that Innocent got this and the evils of wives (I, 17) from John of Salisbury's *Polycraticus*.

result of original sin, and full knowledge of the truth could come only in eternity when man was fully in harmony with God. Human knowledge in this transitory world was therefore clouded and murky. True, saints and mystics might experience great illuminations, but these were ineffable. Real knowledge came through revelation, which meant it was in the Bible and in the received faith of the Church. The first and best object of knowledge (so they usually thought) was one's self: but self-knowledge meant knowing that one was sinful and imperfect. Nonetheless, medieval men believed that shadowy and imperfect glimpses of the truth were available. Man's reason, though clouded with sin, had still the capacity to use logic and understand in part what was true and right. The Bible was revealed truth. Then there was nature itself—numbers, colors, and objects symbolized truth; the stars, for example, revealed God's governance of the world and could be interpreted by astrology. And such truths could be preserved in books. Thus medieval men grasped hopefully after truth, using revelation and reason. But to claim truth for one's own inventiveness or originality would have been a sin of vainglory; and to aspire to knowledge beyond what was man's rightful province would have been a sin of curiosity. "Clarity" in medieval writing was only a hopeful grasp at an impossible goal; at the same time, the medievals believed that truth, by whomever spoken, came from God.

The arrangement of topics in medieval writing is not "organic" in our modern sense, it is better described as "architectonic." The writer is more a scribe or craftsman than a creator; he is doing something comparable to building a house. Things must hang together, therefore, not because of any "inner" necessity but because there is a suitable way to *put* them together. Thus Innocent organized his work according to traditional formulations; and into each topic he worked appropriate subtopics which follow one another without necessary logical or emotional connections. His aim is to view one indisputable truth from different angles in different ways for a clear, functional purpose. One can see this idea of organization as well in their cathedrals and paintings. To "resolve" or "unify" is never in their minds; they are more intent to match things up, to keep them in bal-

ance and proportion, often in two's and three's. Medieval treatises are therefore likely to strike us either as too helter-skelter
or too structured: Innocent's Book I may seem like a jumble of
dolorous notes on human misery, Book III like a heavily "pro-
grammatic" examination of death and hell. We shall understand
this kind of organization best if we do not think of modern novels
with their "point of view," or modern works of scholarship with
their "controlled arguments"; we come closer to the organizational principle of medieval treatises when we read a stock-
holders' report or a textbook, where topics necessary to be
covered are numbered and labelled and material apportioned
under these headings.

In technique and execution, however, we do find conscious
artistry. Individual sentences may be elaborately embellished
and ornamented; the "art" of prose writing lies here, not in a
total plan or a unified conception. It is the same spirit, perhaps,
which moved medieval men to adorn manuscript books con-
taining utterly diverse works with tiny drawings in the margins
and with elaborately illuminated capital letters, or to adorn
cathedrals with diverse carvings. The ornamentation gave pleasure without in any way diminishing the usefulness or truthful-
ness of the chief design. To us it may seem superfluous: we are
likely to think of ornamental prose as "flowery" and therefore in-
sincere. But seeming sincere was not a medieval preoccupation.
Those who wrote did so to express as best they could a truth they
would transmit; it was up to their readers to grasp that truth, or
to decide if it was heresy. But it made truth more appealing if
the writer decked it out in ornaments, by *amplificatio*, as their
rhetoricians called the procedure.

Hence what are reckoned faults in modern writing are often
virtues in medieval writing. The repetition of an idea with
minor variations would, for example, have been admired. Innocent writes:

Time passes, death draws near. In the eyes of the dying man, a
thousand years are as yesterday, which is past. The future is forever being born, the present forever dying, and what is past is
utterly dead. We are forever dying while we are alive; we only

cease to die when we cease to live. Therefore it is better to die to
life than to live waiting for death, for mortal life is but a living
death. (I, 23)

What makes the passage especially artful is the elaborate parallel-
ism of its sentence structure. Here, embellishment suits the
content perfectly and does not merely adorn it—balance, proportionableness, and correspondence are predominant characteristics of medieval style because they were characteristic of
medieval thought. Synonyms, too, become an ornament used
sometimes in what must seem to us a Rabelaisian manner—
but then Rabelais was himself indebted to a long tradition of
piling up words. Thus Innocent draws his work to a close with
an *O altitudo* of word-choices:

> "There shall be weeping and gnashing of teeth," there shall be
> groaning and wailing, shrieking and flailing of arms and scream-
> ing, screeching and shouting; there shall be fear and trembling,
> toil and trouble, holocaust and dreadful stench, and everywhere
> darkness and anguish; there shall be asperity, cruelty, calamity,
> poverty, distress and utter wretchedness; they will feel an oblivion
> of loneliness and namelessness; there shall be twistings and piercings,
> bitterness, terror, hunger and thirst, cold and hot, brimstone and
> fire burning, forever and ever world without end. (III, 20)

The passage illustrates another quality which ornaments many
of Innocent's sentences—alliteration. It shows an influence from
the medieval tradition of rhythmical Latin prose. It shows, too,
the love of variation which occurs not alone in vocabulary but
in constructions: "But let him understand that he is guilty in
his hardness, and hardened in guilt . . ." (I, 25). We even get
sentences like this: "Thus justly does He tell what is just. For
some seek justice with justice, others injustice with injustice; and
some seek justice by unjust means, while others seek injustice by
just means" (II, 3) .

Such qualities of the work, we must remember, were familiar
to learned readers. They do not show that the author himself
was dour or unsophisticated—contemporary accounts make it
plain that in private life Innocent was schooled in the niceties

of high-born conduct, affable, and humorous. They show only
that the serious style of learned discourse, of which he was a
master, has since come to seem inflated. To Chaucer, at any rate,
the stylized rhetoric of medieval schools seemed so; he parodied
it hilariously in the Nun's Priest's Tale. But all this we must forget. It is easy to imagine Innocent writing his rhetorical flights
and passages of highly wrought ornamentation, his "amplifica-
tions" and "apostrophes," with tongue in cheek; but we are
more than two centuries too early for that. The work was
written in earnest, and for five centuries it was read as a classic.
If we read it as men of the Middle Ages and Renaissance did,
we shall have to remember that behind its rhetoric lay a profound vision of human wretchedness and emptiness; and that
behind this lay a vision, equally clear, of man's dignity as God's
creature and his hope of salvation.

ON THE MISERY OF THE
HUMAN CONDITION · *De miseria*
humane conditionis

PROLOGUE

*To my dear lord and father, Peter, by the grace of God bishop
of Porto and the Church of St. Rufina;* Lothario, unworthy cardi-
nal-deacon of SS. Sergus and Bachus, wishes grace in the present
and glory in the future:

I lately took a bit of rest during my many troubles, the occasion
of which you know;[1] but I did not spend this time in complete
idleness. Rather, to put down pride, the chief of all vices, I under-
took to write, as best I could, something about the vileness of the
human condition. This little work I have dedicated to you, ask-
ing only that if your keen mind find in it anything worthwhile,
you attribute all to divine grace. Yet if your lordship approve
it, I will henceforth, with Christ's favor, describe also the dignity
of human nature; so that, as in the present work the proud man
is brought low, in that the humble man will be exalted.

[1] Pope Celestine III (1191–1198) relieved Lothario of his duties as
cardinal; Celestine was a member of the Orsini family, rivals of Lothario's
family. See Introduction, p. xxi f.

BOOK ONE: The Miserable Entrance upon the Human Condition

I ·

Of the Miserable Entrance upon the Human Condition

"Why did I come out of my mother's womb to see labor and sorrow, and that my days should be spent in confusion?"[1] If he said such things of himself, he whom the Lord sanctified in the womb, what am I to say of myself, whom my mother conceived in sin? Ah me, I shall have to say, Mother, why did you conceive me, son of bitterness and sorrow? "Why did I not die in the womb? Having come forth from the womb, why did I not perish immediately? Why was I taken up on the knees? Why was I nursed at the breast?"[2] born to be "burnt and to be fuel for the fire?"[3] "Would that I had been slain in the womb so that my mother might have been my grave and her womb an everlasting conception."[4] "For I should have been as if I had not been, brought from the womb to the tomb."[5]

Who, then, will give my eyes a font of tears to weep the miserable entrance upon the human condition, the guilty progress of human ways, and the damnable exit of a human passing? Wherefore with tears in my eyes I shall take up first what a man is made of; second, what man does; and finally what man is to

---

1 Jer. 20:18.
2 Job 3:11–12.
3 Isa. 9:5.
4 Jer. 20:17.
5 Job 10:19.

be. For sure man was formed out of earth, conceived in guilt, born to punishment. What he does is depraved and illicit, is shameful and improper, vain and unprofitable. He will become fuel for the eternal fires, food for worms, a mass of rottenness.

I shall try to make my explanation clearer and my treatment fuller. Man was formed of dust, slime, and ashes; what is even more vile, of the filthiest seed. He was conceived from the itch of the flesh, in the heat of passion and the stench of lust, and worse yet, with the stain of sin. He was born to toil, dread, and trouble; and more wretched still, was born only to die. He commits depraved acts by which he offends God, his neighbor, and himself; shameful acts by which he defiles his name, his person, and his conscience; and vain acts by which he ignores all things important, useful, and necessary. He will become fuel for those fires which are forever hot and burn forever bright; food for the worm which forever nibbles and digests; a mass of rottenness which will forever stink and reek.

II ·

Of the Vile Matter from which Man Is Made

"Therefore the Lord God formed man from the slime of the earth,"[1] an element having lesser dignity than others. For God made the planets and stars from fire, the breeze and winds from air, the fishes and birds from water; but He made men and beasts from earth.[2] Thus a man, looking upon sea life, will find himself low; looking upon creatures of the air he will know he is lower; and looking upon the creatures of fire he will see he is lowest of all. Nor can he equal heavenly things, nor dare put himself above the earthly; for he finds himself on a level with the beasts and knows he is like them.

"Therefore the death of man and the beast is the same, and the condition of them both is equal, and man has nothing more

[1] Gen. 2:7.

[2] Earth, water, air, and fire, the four elements, were thought to be in a hierarchical order.

than the beast. Of earth they were made, and into earth they return together."[3] These are not just the words of any man, but of wisest Solomon. What then is a man but slime and ashes? Man addresses God: "Remember, I beseech thee, that thou hast made me as the clay, and thou wilt bring me into dust again."[4] And God addresses man: "Dust thou art, and unto dust thou shalt return."[5] "I am compared to mud and am likened to embers and ashes."[6] Now, mud is made of water and dirt, both remaining what they are; but ashes are made of fire and wood, both being consumed. In this a mystery is revealed, but it will be expounded elsewhere. Therefore, mud, why art thou proud? dust, what hast thou to boast about? ashes, why art thou so insolent?

But perhaps you will reply that although Adam himself was formed of the earth's slime *you* were conceived of human seed. On the contrary, Adam was formed of earth, but of virgin earth; you were made of seed, and that unclean. "For who can make clean what was conceived from unclean seed?"[7] "What is man that he should be without spot, and he that is born of a woman that he should appear just?"[8] "Behold, I was conceived in iniquities and in sins did my mother conceive me."[9] Not in one sin alone, not in one transgression alone, but in many sins and many transgressions: in her own sins and transgressions, and the sins and transgressions of others.

III ·

Of the Conception of Children

There is, moreover, a double conception—of seeds, and of natures. The first is an act, the second its result. The parents'

3 Eccles. 3:19–20.
4 Job 10:9.
5 Gen. 3:19.
6 Job 30:19.
7 Job 14:4.
8 Job 15:14.
9 Ps. 50:7.

act is first; and the child inherits its result, which is second. Everyone knows that intercourse, even between married persons, is never performed without the itch of the flesh, the heat of passion, and the stench of lust. Whence the seed conceived is fouled, smirched, corrupted, and the soul infused into it inherits the guilt of sin, the stain of evil-doing, that primeval taint.[1] Just as drink is polluted by a soiled vessel, anything that touches something polluted becomes polluted.

For the soul has three natural powers: the rational, to tell good from evil; the irascible, to repulse the evil; and the concupiscible, to yearn for the good. These three powers are originally corrupted by three opposing vices. The rational power is corrupted by ignorance, so that the soul no longer knows good from evil; the irascible power by rage, so that the soul rejects goodness; and the concupiscible power by lust, so that the soul yearns for evil. Ignorance begets moral turpitude; lust begets sin; and rage begets both turpitude and sin. For it is turpitude not to do those things which we ought to have done, and it is sin to do those things which we ought not to have done.

Now these three vices are got from the corrupt flesh through three fleshly enticements. In carnal intercourse the mind's clarity is put to sleep, whence ignorance is sown; the itch of desire is aroused, from which comes rage; and the desire for pleasure is appeased, from which rises habitual lust. This is the tyranny of the flesh, the law of our members, sin's tinderbox, our nature's sluggardry, chief nourisher of Death, without which no man comes into the world or goes forth. And if as sometimes happens a man escape this culpability, yet it remains, innate and immanent. "For if we say that we have no sin, we deceive ourselves and the truth is not in us."[2]

O heavy necessity, o unhappy condition! Before we sin we are already chained to sin; before guilty, we are guilt's prisoner.

---

[1] The notion that original sin is transmitted by sexual intercourse was common in medieval times. The point was taken up at the Council of Trent (1546): original sin, it was decided, is transmitted rather by the generation of a human *nature* from the stock of Adam. See Denzinger-Bannwart-Umberg, *Enchiridion Symbolorum* (Frigurgi Brisgoviae, 1937), nos. 790, 791; and St. Thomas Aquinas, *Summa Contra Gentiles* IV. 52. (16).

[2] I John 1:8.

"Through one man sin came into this world and through sin death has come over all men."[3] Have not "the fathers eaten a sour grape and the teeth of the children are set on edge?"[4]

IV ·

What Kind of Food Nourishes the Child in
the Womb

Hear now on what food the child is fed in the womb: actually on menstrual blood, which ceases in the female after conception so that the child in her womb will be nourished by it. And this blood is reckoned so detestable and impure that on contact with it fruits will fail to sprout, orchards go dry, herbs wither, the very trees let go their fruit; if a dog eat of it, he goes mad. When a child is conceived, he contracts the defect of the seed, so that lepers and monsters are born of this corruption. Wherefore according to the Mosaic law a woman during her monthly period is considered unclean, and if anyone approach a menstruous woman it is commanded that he be put to death. Because of this uncleanness it is further commanded that a woman keep away from the entrance to the temple for forty days if she bear a male child but for eighty days if she bear a female.

V ·

Of the Helplessness of Children

"Why is light given to him that is in misery and life to them that are in bitterness of soul?"[1] Happy are those who die before they are born, who suffer death before they know life. For some poor souls are born so deformed and unnatural that they seem not

3 Rom. 5:12.
4 Jer. 31:29.
1 Job 3:20.

human but abhominations; perhaps they would have been better off if they had never appeared on the scene at all, because these monsters are so *demonstrable*, are shown off as freaks. Many are born with dwarfed limbs or without all their senses, a sorrow to friends, a disgrace to parents, an embarrassment to relatives.

And yet why do I single out these, when everyone is born without knowledge, speech, or strength? Weeping, without strength, helpless, we are little more than brutes, yea, in some ways less: brutes walk immediately after they are born, but we do not walk erect on our feet or even crawl on our hands and knees.

VI ·

*Of the Pain of Childbirth and the Weeping
of Infants*

Then, too, we are all born weeping to express the misery of our nature. It is observed that the boy cries "Ah" just after birth, the girl cries "E". Whence the common verse:

> They are crying "E" or "Ah",
> All of them born of E-va.

For what is the name "Eva," when examined carefully, but *Eu!* plus *Ah!*—these words being interjections of sorrow or great pain. For this reason, before the Fall the female was called "wo-man" ("made from man"), but after the Fall she deserved to be called "Eva"; and it was said to her, "In sorrow shall you bring forth children."[1]

For there is really no sorrow or pain like that of a woman in labor. Rachel died from the excessive pain of childbirth and while dying named her son Benoni, that is, son of pain. The wife of Phineas, undergoing the pain that came over her, gave

---

[1] Gen. 3:16. The fanciful etymology is typical; see Introduction, p. xxxvi–xxxvii. *Eu + a* did indeed spell "Eva," *u* and *v* being interchangeable. For "woman" the Latin has *virago*, supposedly from Latin *vir* (man).

birth just as she died, and in the very moment of death named
her son Ichabod, that is, son of grief. "But a woman, like a
shipwrecked person, has sorrow when she is bearing; but when
she has given birth to the child, she does not remember the pain
because of the joy that a man is born into the world."[2] Thus she
conceives the child with uncleanness and stench, bears him with
sorrow and pain, nourishes him with toil and trouble, and
watches over him without ceasing, always in fear.

VII ·

*On the Nakedness and the Clothing of an
Infant*

We come naked into the world, and we go naked hence. We
arrive poor and go away poor. "Naked," he said, "did I come
forth from my mother's womb and naked shall I return thither."[1]
"We brought nothing into this world, and certainly we can
carry nothing out."[2]

Or, if it may be said that one enters clothed, listen to the kind
of clothing he wears—foul to speak of, fouler to hear of, foulest
to see: a stinking caul dripping blood. This is the "enclosure"
of which Thamar said, when giving birth, "Why is the enclosure
divided for thee?"[3] And for this reason she called his name
Phares, which means "division."

VIII ·

What Kind of Fruit a Man Produces

O vile indignity of the human condition, O undignified con-

2 John 16:21.
1 Job 1:21.
2 I Tim. 6:7.
3 Gen. 38:29.

dition of man's vileness! Look at the plants and the trees—they produce flowers, foliage, and fruit; you produce nits, lice, and tapeworms. They pour forth oil, wine, and balsam; you give off spit, urine, and dung. They breathe forth a sweet odor; you give off a dreadful stench. As the tree is, so is the fruit, for the bad tree cannot bring forth good fruit, nor the good tree bad fruit. And after all what is the shape of a man but a tree turned upside down? Its roots are the hair, its bole is the head and neck, its trunk the chest and belly, its branches the arms and legs, its foliage the fingers and joints. This is the leaf which is carried off by the wind, the straw dried by the sun.

IX ·

Of the Shortness of this Life

At the very beginning of the human condition we read of men who lived nine hundred years and more. But little by little, as the life of man became shorter, the Lord said to Noah, "My spirit shall not remain in man forever because he is flesh, and his days shall be a hundred and twenty years."[1] This can be applied both to the end of life and to the time for repenting. Very rarely since then do you read of men living longer; and because human life has become shorter and shorter, the psalmist said, "The sum of our years is seventy, and if we are stronger, eighty years, and most of them are labor and sorrow."[2]

But now my short time will end soon. "Our days pass away more quickly than the web is cut by the weaver."[3] "Man born of a woman, living for a short time, is filled with many miseries. He comes forth like a flower and is destroyed and passes as a shadow and never continues in the same state."[4] Few now live to be sixty, and very few live to be seventy years of age.

[1] Gen. 6:3.
[2] Ps. 89:10.
[3] Job 7:6.
[4] Job 14:1–2.

X ·

Of the Discomfort of Old Age

But even then, if anyone does reach old age, his heart weakens, his head shakes, his vigor wanes, his breath reeks, his face is wrinkled and his back bent, his eyes grow dim and his joints weak, his nose runs, his hair falls out, his hand trembles and he makes silly gestures, his teeth decay, and his ears get stopped with wax. An old man is easily provoked and hard to calm down. He will believe anything and question nothing. He is stingy and greedy, gloomy, querulous, quick to speak, slow to listen, though by no means slow to anger. He praises the good old days and hates the present, curses modern times, lauds the past, sighs and frets, falls into a stupor, and gets sick. Hear what the poet says:

Many discomforts surround an old man.[1]

But then the old cannot glory over the young any more than the young can scorn the old. For we are what they once were; and some day we will be what they are now.

XI ·

Of Mortals' Toil

A bird is born to fly; man is born to toil. All his days are full of toil and hardship, and at night his mind has no rest. And is this not vanity? There is nothing under the sun to be had without toil, nothing under the moon without its waning, nothing in time without vanity. For time is but the duration of the motion of mutable things.

1 Horace, *Ars Poetica* 169.

"Vanity of vanities," says Ecclesiastes, "and all is vanity."[1] O how varied are the pursuits of man, how diverse his practices. But all have one end and the same result: toil and vexation of spirit. "Great labor is created for all men and a heavy yoke is upon the children of Adam, from the day of their coming out of their mother's womb until the day of their burial into the mother of all."[2]

XII ·

Of Varied Pursuits of the Wise

Let wise men seek out and study the height of the sky, the breadth of the earth, and the depth of the sea. Let them dispute about each, let them examine all, let them learn and teach as long as they want. What do they have for their efforts but toil, sorrow, and vexation of spirit? He knew this from experience who said, "And I had given my heart to know prudence, and learning, and errors and folly, and I perceived that it was labor and vexation of spirit, because in much wisdom there is much imagination, and he who adds knowledge adds labor."[1]

For although a researcher must toil through many vigils and keep vigil over his toils, there is hardly anything so cheap and easy that a man can understand it fully and clearly, unless perhaps he knows for sure that *nothing* is known for sure. This may seem an unresolvable contradiction. But why? "For the corruptible body is a load upon the soul, and the earthly habitation presses down upon the mind that muses on many things."[2] Hear what Solomon says about this: "All things are hard; man cannot explain them by word."[3] "For there are some that day and night take no sleep with their eyes, and can find no reason for all the

1 Eccles. 1:2.
2 Ecclus. 40:1.
1 Eccles. 1:17–18.
2 Wisd. 9:15.
3 Eccles. 1:8.

works of God, and the more he shall labor to seek, so much the
less shall he find."[4]

"The searchers have failed in their search, because man shall
come to a deep heart, and God shall be exalted."[5] "He who is
a searcher of majesty shall be overwhelmed by glory."[6] The man
who knows more doubts more; he *seems* to know more who is
the more a fool. Therefore it is a part of wisdom to know what
you do not know. "God made man right, but he has entangled
himself in an infinity of questions."[7]

XIII ·

Of the Varied Interests of Men

We mortals clamber over hedges and poke around paths, hike up
hills, climb mountains, scale cliffs, practically fly over the Alps;
people walk right over pits and into caves; they pry into the
bowels of the earth, the depths of the sea, the hidden windings
of rivers, the darkness of the forest, the pathless desert.[1] They
endure wind and pelting rain, thunder and lightning, tempests,
the heaving of the flood, catastrophe, disaster. They hammer
metals and melt them, carve and polish stones, fell timber and
hew it; they set the loom and weave, cut and sew garments, build
houses and plant gardens, till the soil, cultivate the vineyard;
they kindle ovens, they build mills, they fish, hunt, and trap
birds.

Or else they meditate and ponder, consult each other and get
things settled, complain and sue each other, plunder and pilfer,

4 Eccles. 8:16–17.
5 Ps. 63:7–8.
6 Prov. 25:27.
7 Eccles. 7:30.

1 An interesting passage, since it is often thought that medieval men had
no interest in scenery, mountain-climbing, sightseeing, and the like;
Petrarch's ascent of Mt. Ventoux, for example, is often thought a great
departure from medieval indifference to nature.

cheat, finagle, quarrel, fight; do almost anything to heap up riches, increase profits, and struggle for any financial advantage; win honors, raise their rank, extend their powers. And all this, too, is but toil and vexation of mind.

If you do not believe me, believe Solomon. "I made me," he said, "great works. I built me houses and planted vineyards. I made gardens and orchards and set them with trees of all kinds. I made ponds of water to water therewith the wood of the young trees. I got menservants and maidservants and had a great family, and herds of oxen and great flocks of sheep, above all who were before me in Jerusalem. I heaped together for myself silver and gold, the wealth of kings and provinces. I got singing men and singing women and the delights of the sons of men, cups and vessels for pouring wine, and I surpassed in wealth all who were before me in Jerusalem. And when I turned myself to all the works which my hands had wrought, and the labors at which I had worked in vain, I saw in all things vanity, and vexation of mind, and that nothing was lasting under the sun"[2] which was not toil and vexation of spirit.

XIV ·

Of Various Anxieties

How much anxiety tortures mortals! They suffer all kinds of cares, are burdened with worry, tremble and shrink with fears and terrors, are weighted down with sorrow. Their nervousness makes them depressed, and their depression makes them nervous. Rich or poor, master or slave, married or single, good and bad alike—all suffer worldly torments and are tormented by worldly vexations. Believe, then, a knowing teacher: "And if I be wicked, woe unto me, and if I be just, I shall not lift up my head, being filled with affliction and misery."[1]

2 Eccles. 2:4–9, 11.
1 Job 10:15.

XV ·

Of the Misery of the Rich and Poor

The poor, for example, go without food; they suffer hardship, hunger, thirst, cold, nakedness; they become worthless, they waste away; people despise and humiliate them. O wretched condition of the begger! If he begs, he is ashamed; if he begs not, he is needy and *must* beg. He claims God is unjust because He does not distribute things fairly; he accuses his neighbor of malice because he does not help him; and so he gets angry, grumbles, and curses.

Listen then to the words of the wise man: "It is better to die than to want."[1] "Even to his neighbor shall the poor man be hateful."[2] "All the days of the poor man are evil."[3] "The brethren of the poor man hate him; also his friends have departed far from him."[4]

> You will have friends enough when fortune is fair,
> But if the weather turns dark, friends become rare.[5]

For shame! A person is valued according to his wealth, when wealth should be valued according to the person: a man is thought as good as he is rich, and as bad as he is poor—but we should think him as rich as he is good, and as poor as he is bad.

And yet, the rich man is debauched by his own abundance, an unbridled boaster who runs about at will, and so runs afoul into immorality. What had been the delights of his wrongs become the instruments of his punishment. Toil in acquiring, fear in possessing, and sorrow in losing make him weary, dis-

---

[1] Ecclus. 40:29.
[2] Prov. 14:20.
[3] Prov. 15:15.
[4] Prov. 19:7.
[5] Ovid, *Tristia* I. ix. 5–6.

traught, always uneasy. "Where your treasure is, there is also your heart."[6] But of this we will speak more fully later.[7]

XVI ·

Of the Misery of Serfs and Masters

The serf is terrified of threats, wearied with service, and a ready subject for beatings. Money is extorted from him which, if he have it not, he is compelled to get; and of which, if he have it, he is at once deprived. What is the master's fault becomes the serf's punishment; but the serf's fault is the master's prey.

> Whatever folly their kings commit,
> The Greeks must pay for all of it.[1]

"The wild ass in the desert is the lion's prey."[2] So the poor are the food of the rich. O wretched condition of servitude! "Nature bore them free,"[3] but Fortune made them slaves. The serf is forced into suffering, and no one is allowed to pity him; he is forced into pain, and no one may show sympathy. He is not his own master, so no one is on his side. By the same token, wretched are those in military service, for it is miserable "to live at another's table."[4]

And, if the master is cruel, he must fear his subjects' profligacy; if he is gentle, he is bound to be despised because of his subjects' insolence. Fear is the lot of the severe master, insult of the kind-hearted one. For cruelty breeds hate and familiarity breeds contempt: familial care wears him down, the worries of the household keep him vexed. He must always be prepared and at all times warned to stay clear of evildoers' tricks, beat off at-

---

6 Matt. 6:21.
7 In Book III, especially chapter xiii.
1 Horace, *Epistles* I. ii. 14.
2 Ecclus. 13:23.
3 St. Gregory, *Regula Pastoralis* II. 6.
4 Juvenal, *Satires* V. 2.

tackers, destroy enemies, and guard his people. Nor is the evil
of the day sufficient thereunto, but day brings up the day's labor
and night makes known night's cares. Thus masters spend the
day in toil and pass the night in sleeplessness.

XVII ·

Of the Misery of Married and Single People

Only as fire does not burn, does flesh not lust; for no matter how
much it be fought off, that Jebusite will never really be driven
out:

> You may drive nature out with a pitchfork,
> but she will come back again.[1]

"Not all," He said, "can accept this teaching. Let him accept it
who can."[2] When God gave orders about certain priestly vest-
ments with which Moses should clothe Aaron and his sons, He
did not give instructions just about girdles, but that they should
wear girdles when they entered the tabernacle of the Covenant.[3]
Even the Apostle says, "Do not deprive each other, except perhaps by consent for a time, that you may give yourselves to
prayer, and return together again lest Satan tempt you for your
incontinency."[4] "For it is better to marry than to burn."[5]

Therefore the messenger of Satan fights against continence.
He goads the flesh and sorely buffets the soul, kindles the fire of
nature with the bellows of suggestion, puts fuel thereto, gives us

---

[1] Horace, *Epistles* I. x. 24.

[2] Matt. 19:12.

[3] The point is probably that the girdle symbolizes righteousness of a
specifically high degree and to which only a few are called. Marriage was
considered a lesser degree of perfection than widowhood or virginity. On
perfection see Morton W. Bloomfield, *Franciscan Studies*, XVII (1957),
229–232.

[4] I Cor. 7:5.

[5] I Cor. 7:9.

the ability, and provides the opportunity. Good looks, which are seen fast enough and easy to lust for, also militate against continence. When David went out for a walk after noon in the sun porch of the royal palace, seeing Bersabee washing herself nearby, for she was a right beautiful woman, he sent and took her and slept with her.

Furthermore, a married man is concerned and quite of two minds about the things of the world. For he is distracted by many troubles and all cut up by his worries: to provide for needs of his children and wife, his menservants and maidservants. "For such shall have tribulation of the flesh."[6]

The wife insists on having precious jewels and a huge wardrobe, so that her attire often costs more than her husband's salary; but otherwise she sighs and weeps, babbles and murmurs day and night. There are three things which keep a man from staying home: smoke, a leaky roof, and a shrewish wife. "This woman," she says, "goes out better dressed, that one is honored by everybody; but poor little me, I'm the only one in the whole group of women that they scorn—they all look down their noses at me." She wants all his attention and all his praise; if he praises another she takes it as a humiliation. He must like everything she likes, hate everything she spurns. She wants to master, and will not be mastered. She will not be a servant, *she* must be in charge. She must have a finger in everything. If she be beautiful, men readily go after her; if she be ugly, she goes as readily after them. It is hard to keep what many want, and annoying to have what no one cares about. One man is attracted by a woman's figure, another by her charm or humor or personality; one way or another she is taken, since she is besieged on all sides.[7]

When you buy a horse, an ass, an ox, a dog, clothes and a bed, even a cup and a pitcher, you first get a chance to look them over. But no one displays a bride, lest she displease before the marriage; whatever her condition one takes her as she is. No matter if she be ugly or foul-smelling, if she be sick or foolish, if she be

6 I Cor. 7:28.

7 Cf. St. Jerome, *Against Jovinian* I. 47. The passage is an interesting view of the reputedly low position of women in medieval life.

proud or easily angered, or if she have any vicious trait; only for
adultery can a man put away his wife. And even then, he who
divorces cannot marry another, nor can a divorced woman either.
For everyone who "puts away his wife, except for the cause of
fornication, and marries another, commits adultery, and he that
shall marry her that is put away commits adultery."[8] But if a
wife leave her husband, she must remain unmarried or be
reconciled to him; the same is true for a man if he leave his wife.

So the burden of marriage is heavy indeed, for "He that keeps
an adulteress is foolish and wicked,"[9] and he is the very pro-
tector of shame who conceals his wife's crime. But if he put away
the adulteress he is punished for no fault of his own, since while
she is alive he is forced to be continent. On this account the disciples said to Christ, "If this is the case with a man and his wife,
it is not expedient to marry."[10] Who could ever just calmly put
up with a rival? Suspicion alone tortures the jealous man, for
although it is written, "They shall be two in one flesh,"[11] a man's
jealousy will scarcely tolerate two men in the flesh of one
woman.[12]

XVIII ·

Of the Misery of the Good and the Evil

It is not for the wicked to rejoice, says the Lord, "For by what
things a man sins, by the same also he is tormented."[1] For the
worm of conscience never dies, and reason's light is never put
out. "I have seen those who work iniquity and sow sorrows and

8 Matt. 5:32.
9 Prov. 18:22.
10 Matt. 19:10.
11 Gen. 2:24.
12 The whole passage is a conventional anti-feminist utterance. See Francis
Lee Utley, *The Crooked Rib* (Columbus, Ohio: Ohio State University Press,
1944).
1 Wisd. 11:17.

reap them perishing by the blast of God and consumed by the spirit of His wrath."[2] Pride inflates, envy gnaws, avarice goads, wrath inflames, gluttony chokes, lechery destroys, lying ensnares, murder defiles. So, too, other vices have their portents, for the sinful delights which entice men are the very instruments of God's punishment. "The envious man loses weight when he sees someone else getting fat."[3] But,

> The tyrants of Sicily never discovered a worse form of torment than envy.[4]

For vice corrupts nature as the Apostle witnesses: "Because they have become vain in their thoughts, and their foolish hearts have been darkened, therefore God gave them up to the desires of their hearts unto uncleanness, to dishonor their own bodies, and as they liked not to have God in their knowledge, God delivered them up to a reprobate sense, to do those things which are not convenient."[5]

But even those "who will to live godly in Christ Jesus will suffer persecution."[6] "The saints had the experience of mockery and stripes, yes, even of chains and prisons. They were stoned, they were cut asunder, they were tempted, they were put to death by the sword for the Lord. They went about in sheepskins and goatskins, being in want, distressed, and afflicted, of whom the world was not worthy, wandering in deserts, in mountains, and in dens and in caves of the earth."[7] "In peril from floods, in peril from robbers, in peril from the gentiles, in peril from the city, in peril from false brethren. In labor and hardship, in many watchings, in hunger and thirst, in fastings often, in cold and nakedness,"[8] in many hardships.

For the just man "denies himself,"[9] crucifying his body on

---

2 Job 4:8–9.
3 Horace, *Epistles* I. ii. 56.
4 *Ibid.,* 57–59.
5 Rom. 1:21, 24, 28.
6 II Tim. 3:12.
7 Heb. 11:36–38.
8 II Cor. 11:26–27.
9 Luke 9:23.

the cross of its own vices and concupiscences, so that the world
is crucified to him and he to the world. He does not have in this
life a lasting city of this world, but seeks the future city of God.
He endures the world as an exile, shut up in the body as in a
prison. "I am a sojourner on the earth"[10] "and a pilgrim like all
my fathers. Turn thy eyes from me, that I may recover, before I go
and am no more."[11] "Woe is me that my sojourning is prolonged;
I have dwelt with the inhabitants of Cedar, my soul has long
been a sojourner."[12] "Who is weak and I am not weak? Who is
scandalized and I am not on fire?"[13] For the sins of those about
us are a torment to the righteous. And this teaching is the flowing water which Caleb gave for dowry to his daughter Axa.

XIX ·

On the Enemies of Man

"The life of man on the earth is a warfare."[1] Is it not truly warfare when a manifold enemy—the devil and man, the world and
the flesh—always and everywhere lie in wait to sieze us, follow
us about to slay us?—the world through the four elements, the
flesh through the senses, man through the beasts, and the devil
through vices. "For the flesh lusts against the spirit and the
spirit against the flesh."[2] For "our wrestling is not against flesh
and blood, but against principalities and powers, against the
rulers of the world of darkness."[3] "For your adversary the devil,
as a roaring lion, goes about seeking whom he may devour."[4]

The fiery darts of the most wicked one are kindled. Death

10 Ps. 118:19.
11 Ps. 38:13–14.
12 Ps. 119:5.
13 II Cor. 11:29.

1 Job 7:1.
2 Gal. 5:17.
3 Eph. 6:12.
4 I Pet. 5:8.

enters through windows. The eye ravishes the soul. The terrestrial orb itself fights against the unwise: nation against nation, kingdom against kingdom, here and there dreadful earthquakes, plagues and famines, tempests, and the very terrors of the sky. Earth produces thorns and thistles; water produces storms and waves; air produces tempests and thunder; fire produces fireballs and lightning. "Cursed is the earth in thy work," He said. "Thorns and thistles shall it bring forth to thee. In the sweat of thy face shalt thou eat thy bread, until thou return to the earth, for dust thou art and unto dust thou shalt return."[5]

"The boar out of the wood has laid it waste and a singular wild beast has devoured it."[6] The wolf and bear, the panther and lion, the tiger and wild ass, the crocodile and griffin; the serpent and the snake, the lizard and the asp, the horned serpent, the dragon, the scorpion, the viper; nits, fleas, bugs, lice, gnats, flies, beetles, wasps, fishes and birds. For we who were created to be lords over the fishes of the sea and the birds of the sky and over all living things that move upon the face of the earth, now are given over to them for prey, and are become their food. For it is written: "I will send the teeth of beasts upon them, with the fury of creatures that trail upon the ground, and of serpents."[7]

XX ·

Why the Body Is Called the Prison of the Soul

"Unhappy man that I am! Who will deliver me from the body of this death?"[1] Surely he does not want to be let out of prison who does not want to leave his body, for the body is the soul's prison. Of this the psalmist speaks: "Bring my soul out of prison."[2] Nowhere is there rest and quiet, nowhere peace and

[5] Gen. 3:17–19.
[6] Ps. 79:14.
[7] Deut. 32:24.
[1] Rom. 7:24.
[2] Ps. 141:8.

security; everywhere is fear and trembling, toil and trouble. The flesh is troubled during life, and the soul will bemourn itself.

XXI ·

On the Brevity of Joy

What man has ever spent even one whole day joyfully in his pleasure, undisturbed in some part of the day by a guilty conscience or a flash of anger or the motion of concupiscence; unshaken by envious spite or hot avarice or swelling pride; untroubled by some loss, offense, or suffering; and, last, unbothered by some sight, sound, or action? He would be

A bird as rare on the earth as a black swan.[1]

Hear this saying of the wise man: "From the morning to the evening the time shall be changed."[2] Vain thoughts fall one upon another and the mind is led astray in diverse ways. "They take the timbrel and the harp and rejoice at the sound of the organ. They spend their days in wealth and in a moment they go down to hell."[3]

XXII ·

On Unexpected Sorrow

For sudden sorrow always follows worldly joy: what begins in gaiety ends in grief. Worldly happiness is besprinkled indeed with much bitterness. He knew this who said, "Laughter shall be mingled with sorrow, and mourning takes hold of the end of joy."[1] The children of Job experienced it when they ate and

1 Juvenal, *Satires* VI. 165.
2 Ecclus. 18:26.
3 Job 21:12–13.
1 Prov. 14:13.

drank wine in the house of their first-born brother, for suddenly a strong wind rushed out of the desert and struck the four corners of the house, which fell in and crushed them all. Rightly then did the father say, "My harp is tuned to mourning and my organ into the voice of those that weep."[2]

"It is better to go into the house of mourning than to go into the house of feasting."[3] A wise counsel: "In the day of good things, be not unmindful of evil things."[4] "In all thy works remember thy last end and thou shalt never sin."[5]

XXIII •

On the Nearness of Death

A man's last day is always the first in importance, but his first day is never considered his last. Yet it is fitting to live always on this principle, that one should act as if in the moment of death. For it is written: "Remember that death is not slow."[1] Time passes, death draws near. In the eyes of the dying man a thousand years are as yesterday, which is past. The future is forever being born, the present forever dying, and what is past is utterly dead. We are forever dying while we are alive; we only cease to die when we cease to live. Therefore it is better to die to life than to live waiting for death, for mortal life is but a living death.

Whence Solomon said, "I praised the dead rather than the living, and I judged him happier than them both who is not yet born."[2] Life flees quickly and cannot be called back; but death follows on our heels and cannot be held off. This is the marvel: that as life grows longer it grows shorter, for as it moves on, it moves toward its end.

2 Job 30:31.
3 Eccles. 7:3.
4 Ecclus. 11:27.
5 Ecclus. 7:40.

1 Ecclus. 14:12.
2 Eccles. 4:2-3.

XXIV ·

On the Terror of Dreams

In the time set aside for rest we get no rest; dreams frighten us, sudden images trouble us. And although the things dreamers dream are not really depressing or terrible or burdensome, still sleepers *are* really depressed and terrified and wearied: sometimes they cry in their sleep and often awake upset. But if they dream something pleasant, they awake no less saddened because they have lost it.

Hear what Eliphaz the Themanite says on this subject: "In the horror of a vision by night, when deep sleep is wont to hold man, fear seized me and trembling, and all my bones were frightened, and when a spirit passed before me, the hair of my flesh stood up."[1] Hear, too, the words of Job: "If I say my bed shall comfort me and I shall be relieved speaking with myself on my couch, thou wilt frighten me with dreams and terrify me with visions."[2] Nebuchadnezzar had a dream which terrified him badly; and the images of his brain troubled him.

Dreaming is born of many cares, so that where there are frequent dreams there are many vanities. Dreams have made great numbers of men do wrong, and have destroyed those who put hope in them. For impure images appear in dreams, and by such nocturnal illusions not only is the flesh soiled, but the soul is spotted.[3] Wherefore the Lord says in Leviticus: "If there be

1 Job 4:13-15.
2 Job 7:13-14.
3 The point was a bone of much contention during the late Middle Ages. By some it was not considered a sin to experience or even be "delighted" by the involuntary movements of sense or such images as might appear in dreams, unless one acted upon such notions with full consent of the will. Others, among them St. Thomas, held that it was a sin of omission to entertain any impure feelings or impulses in any area where reason could hold sway. See O. Lottin, *Psychologie et morale aux XII et XIII siècles* (6 vols. in 8; Louvain: Abbaye du Mont César, 1942–1960), I, 393-424, II, 493-496, 588-589, *et passim*.

among you any man that is defiled in a dream by night, he shall go forth out of the camp, and shall not return before he be washed with water in the evening; and after sunset he shall return into the camp."[4]

XXV ·

On Compassion

What a sorrow disturbs us, what fear strikes us when we sense some harm to friends or fear a danger to relatives! Sometimes a man in good health is more perturbed by fear than a sick man by infirmity. For the former has his troubles voluntarily, whereas the latter has his sickness against his will. So the poet was right when he said,

Love is a thing full of restless fear.[1]

Whose heart is so stony, so made of iron, that he does not heave a sigh or let fall a tear when he sees the illness or death of a neighbor or friend; and who does not pity the sufferer and feel sorry for the bereaved? Jesus Himself, when He saw Mary and the Jews who came with her weeping at the tomb of Lazarus, groaned in spirit, was Himself troubled, and wept. Perhaps not because he died, but rather because He had called the dead man back to the miseries of life. But let him understand that he is guilty in his hardness, and hardened in guilt, who mourns the bodily death of a friend but not the spiritual death of his soul.

XXVI ·

That There Are Innumerable Kinds of Illness

Medical studies over the ages have not yet been able to search

[4] Deut. 23:10–11. "Leviticus" in the text is evidently an error.
[1] Ovid, *Heroides* 1. 12.

out all the different kinds of sickness, all the kinds of suffering that human frailty can endure. Should I say the unendurable suffering of diseases, or insufferable endurance? Better I join them both; it is unendurable because of the harshness of suffering, but it is to be endured out of necessity.

Human nature declines more and more from day to day; thus many things which at one time were healthy experiences today are deadly because of the weakness of nature itself. Each world, macrocosm and microcosm, has already grown old, and the longer the old age of each is drawn out, the more the nature of each is thrown into disorder.

XXVII ·

On Sudden Misfortune

Then, suddenly, when least expected, misfortune strikes, a calamity befalls us, disease attacks; or death, which no one can escape, carries us off. Therefore, "Boast not for tomorrow, for you know not what the day to come may bring forth."[1] "Man knows not his own end; but as fishes are taken with the hook, and as birds are caught with the snare, so men are taken in the evil time when it shall suddenly come upon them."[2]

XXVIII ·

On Varied Forms of Torment

And what am I to say of those wretches who are punished by innumerable kinds of torture?—beaten down with cudgels, slashed at the throat with a sword, burnt with flames, burned alive under stones, mangled by hooks, hung on the gibbet, wrung by man-

1 Prov. 27:1.
2 Eccles. 9:12.

acles and scourged by whips;[1] they are confined in chains and
bruised in dungeons, held in prison and starved, thrown over
precipices and drowned, flayed and dismembered, hacked to
pieces, stabbed in the belly. "Such as are for death, to death;
such as are for the sword, to the sword; such as are for famine, to
famine; such as are for captivity, to captivity."[2] Cruel judgment,
inhuman punishment, sorrowful spectacle; they are given as
food to the birds of the air, the beasts of the earth, the fish in the
sea. Alas! Alas! miserable mothers, to have borne such unhappy
children!

XXIX ·

Of a Certain Horrible Crime:
A Woman Who Ate Her Own Infant

Let me then be permitted to insert that horrible crime which
Josephus describes in his work on the Jewish siege.[1] A certain
woman, wealthy and of noble birth, suffered the common fate
of the siege with the rest of the multitude who had fled to
Jerusalem: the rulers took away all the remnant of wealth she
had brought from home to the city. If there was anything left of
the great riches by which she supported her tenuous daily existence, the robbers' accomplices, breaking in by turns, seized it.
Because of this, one might say she became insane with resent-
ment, so that at times she urged the robbers with curses and cries
to kill her.

But none of them would slay her, either out of cruelty or pity,
and if perhaps she did get some food, others demanded it, and
now there was never a supply equal to the demand; moreover, a
fierce hunger pierced her bowels and the very marrow of her
bones; hunger drove her hard toward madness until, taking the
worst possible counsel, she armed herself against the very laws

[1] Literally "tigers" and "scorpions," presumably medieval instruments
of torture.

[2] Jer. 15:2.

[1] See Josephus, *De Bello Judaico* VI. 3–4.

of nature. For she had at her breast a baby son whom she held before her eyes and said, "O wretched mother, O more wretched son, for whom shall I save you in war, famine, and the thieves' plunder? For even if your life were spared, we would be driven under the yoke of Roman slavery. Come now, therefore, my child, and be food for your mother, madness for the robbers, and a tale for all ages of what alone was missing in the massacre of the Jews." And when she had said this, forthwith she cut the throat of her son. Then she put him over the fire and roasted him, ate half, and kept the other half hid.

Of a sudden, then, the robbers rushed in, having sniffed the odor of roasting meat, and threatened death unless she uncover at once the food she had prepared. She answered, "I have kept the best for you," and immediately showed the members of the baby which were left. Then a terrible horror seized them, and though they had the souls of monsters, they were benumbed and their voices stuck in their throats. But she, more cruel than the robbers themselves, said with a savage expression, "It was I who bore him, he is my son, and it is my crime. Eat what I gave birth to, for I ate of him before you; you need be no more fastidious than his mother, nor softer than a woman. But if some sense of righteousness overcomes you and you spurn my food, I have already fed on it and I will feed on it again." After this the robbers fled in terror, and of all her wealth they left only this food for this wretched mother.

XXX ·

That at Times the Innocent Is Punished
While the Guilty Is Freed

No man should trust that he is free of punishment who knows he is free of guilt.[1] He who stands should see to it that he fall

---

[1] The reference is to the atonement of the Cross, in which Christ took upon himself the *guilt* of original sin; man was left to suffer its punishment in the world.

not. For often the innocent man is condemned and the guilty man set free; the pious man is punished, the impious honored; Jesus is crucified, Barabbas set free. And indeed, these days the quiet man is thought useless, the religious man is thought a hypocrite, and the simple man is thought a fool. "The simplicity of the just man is laughed to scorn, the lamp despised in the thoughts of the rich!"[2]

End of Book One

2 Job 12:4–5.

BOOK TWO: The Guilty Progress of the Human Condition

I ·

Of the Guilty Progress of the Human Condition

Men strive especially for three things: riches, pleasures, and honors. Riches lead to immorality, pleasures to shame, and honors to vanity. Hence the Apostle John says, "Do not love the world or the things that are in the world; because all that is in the world is the concupiscence of the flesh and the concupiscence of the eyes and the pride of life."[1] The concupiscence of the flesh pertains to pleasures, the concupiscence of the eyes to riches, and the pride of life to honors. Riches beget covetousness and avarice, pleasures give birth to gluttony and lechery, and honors nourish pride and boasting.

II ·

Of Covetousness

"Nothing is more wicked than a covetous man and there is not a more wicked thing than to love money."[1] That is the statement

[1] John 2:15–16. On this tradition in medieval thought, see Donald R. Howard, *The Three Temptations* (Princeton, N.J.: Princeton University Press, 1966), especially pp. 43–75. Innocent begins with the second temptation, the concupiscence of the eyes—i.e., the love of riches.

[1] Ecclus. 10:9, 10.

of the wise man, and the Apostle confirms it by saying, "They that will become rich fall into temptation and into the snare of the devil and into many unprofitable and hurtful desires, which drown men into destruction and perdition. For the desire of money is the root of all evils."[2] It causes sacrilege and theft, incites robbery and plunder, starts wars and prompts murders; it buys and sells in simony, seeks and takes without fairness, trades and lends without justice, presses with guile and threatens with fraud; it violates agreements and breaks oaths, corrupts witnesses, and perverts judges.

III ·

On Bribery

Consider the words of the evangelical prophet Isaiah: "They all love bribes, they run after rewards, they do not judge for the orphan, and the widow's case does not come before them."[1] Those who pass judgment are not above bribery, for they judge without a love of justice; indeed bribery overruns them, because they judge with a love of money. They are always out for a gift, a promise, or at least a hope; hence they never judge in favor of the orphan, who cannot give or promise, let alone inspire hope.

O faithless princes, companions of thieves, you who love bribes and graft! You will never take your hands off bribes unless you drive covetousness from your hearts. It was of you that the prophet spoke: "Her princes are like wolves seizing the prey, and they run after gain through covetousness."[2] "Her princes have judged for bribes, and her priests have taught for hire, and her prophets foretold for money."[3]

On the other hand, the Lord commanded in the Law, "Thou shalt appoint judges and magistrates in all thy gates, that they

2 I Tim. 6:9–10.

1 Isa. 1:23.
2 Ezech. 22:27.
3 Mich. 3:11.

may judge the people with a just judgment and not go aside to either part. Thou shalt not accept the person nor gifts, for gifts blind the eyes of the wise and change the words of the just. Justly follow after what is just so that you may live."[4] Thus justly does He tell what is just. For some seek justice with justice, others injustice with injustice; and some seek justice by unjust means, while others seek injustice by just means.

IV ·

On Respect of Persons

Woe to you who have been corrupted by pressure or bribery, influenced by love or hate to "call evil good and good evil, who put darkness for light and light for darkness,"[1] killing souls which do not die and giving life to souls which do not live. You pay no attention to the value of a case, but to the value of a person; not to laws but to bribes; not to justice but to money; not to reason's dictates but to your will's desire; not to the law's decree but to your mind's urging. You do not bend your mind to justice, but bend justice to your mind; not in order that you desire what is lawful but that it may be made lawful to do what you desire.[2] For your eye is never so pure as to keep the brightness of the whole body; you add always some yeast that corrupts the whole.[3]

You neglect the poor man's case with delay, promote the rich man's with dispatch; to the poor you are harsh, to the rich mild; you heed the poor but churlishly, then treat the rich with utmost partiality; you only half hear the case of the poor man, but with the rich man miss never a word. The poor man cries out and no one hears; the rich man but parts his lips and all applaud. "The rich man spoke and all held their peace, and what he said they

[4] Deut. 16:18–20.

[1] Isa. 5:20.

[2] A difficult passage; "mind" and "justice" are in reverse order in the Latin. The translation here follows Gascoigne's.

[3] See Introduction, p. xxxvii.

extol even to the clouds; the poor man spoke and they say, 'Who is this?' and if he stumble, they will overthrow him."[4] He who is wronged by force speaks up and no one hears, he cries out and there is none to judge.

If, by chance, you lawyers accept the case of a poor man, you play around with it absent-mindedly; but when you get the case of a rich man, you push it forward persistently. You despise the poor and honor the rich; you rise before the latter with reverence, but you step on the former with contempt. "For if there shall come into your assembly a man having a golden ring, in fine apparel, and there shall come in also a poor man in mean attire, and you have respect for him that is clothed with the fine apparel and shall say to him, 'Sit thou here well,' but shall say to the poor man, 'Stand thou there,' or 'Sit under my footstool,' do you not judge within yourselves and become judges of unjust thoughts?"[5] For the prophet spoke about you and against you: "They are become great and rich, they are grown gross and fat; they have not managed the cause of the fatherless, and they have not judged the judgment of the poor."[6] But in the Law it is commanded: "There shall be no difference of persons; you shall hear the little as well as the great. Neither shall you respect any man's person, because it is the judgment of God."[7] "Because with God there is no respect of persons."[8]

V ·

On the Sale of Justice

You give no favors freely nor render justice justly, for it is not rendered but sold, and not given except for a price. Often you delay justice so long that you take from the litigant more than

[4] Ecclus. 13:28–29.
[5] Jas. 2:2–4.
[6] Jer. 5:27–28.
[7] Deut. 1:17.
[8] Rom. 2:11.

the amount in dispute, your fees being more than the judgment. What will you be able to reply at the last judgment to God, who commanded, "Freely give what you have freely received"?[1] Profit in the bank, loss on your soul: you gain money, but with it gain your soul's captivity. For, "What does it profit a man if he gain the whole world but suffer the loss of his own soul? Or what will a man give in exchange for his soul?"[2] "No brother can redeem, nor shall man redeem. He shall not give to God his ransom nor the price of the redemption of his soul; he shall labor forever and shall still live unto the end."[3] Hear, you rich men, what the Apostle James says against you: "Come now, you rich man, weep and howl in your miseries which will come upon you. Your riches are corrupted and your garments are moth-eaten. Your gold and silver are cankered and the rust of them shall be for a testimony against you, and shall eat your flesh like fire. You have stored up to yourselves wrath against the last days. Behold, the hire of the laborers who reaped your fields, which by fraud has been kept back by you, cries out, and the cry has entered into the ears of the Lord of the Sabaoth."[4] Thus Truth commands, "Do not lay up for yourselves treasures on earth, where rust and moth consume and where thieves break in and steal."[5]

VI ·

On the Insatiable Desire of Covetous Men

Insatiable cupidity is an unquenchable fire. Was there ever a covetous man content with his first wish? When he has got what he wanted, he always longs to have more, and never sets his present possessions as a limit. "The eye of the covetous man is insatiable in his portion of iniquity; he will not be satisfied."[1] "A

1 Matt. 10:8.
2 Matt. 16:26.
3 Ps. 48:8–10.
4 Jas. 5:1–4.
5 Matt. 6:19.
1 Ecclus. 14:9.

covetous man shall not be satisfied with money, and he that loves riches shall reap no fruit from them."[2] Nor Hell nor perdition is ever sated, nor the insatiable eyes of men. "The horseleech has two daughters who say, 'Bring, bring.' "[3] For:

The love of money increases as the pile of coin mounts up.[4]

VII ·

Why the Covetous Cannot Be Satisfied

Would you know, you men of greed, why you are always empty and never full? Hear, then: No measure is full, whatever it hold, which can hold more. Yet the human soul can hold God, for he that clings to the Lord is one in spirit with Him. However much the soul contains, therefore, it is never full unless it hold God, whom it can always hold.

If then, O men of greed, you would be satisfied, leave covetousness: you can never be satisfied as long as you are covetous. There is no meeting of the light with darkness, nor of Christ with Belial; for no one can serve God and Mammon.

VIII ·

On Riches Falsely Named

O false happiness of riches, which in fact make the rich *un*happy. For what is more false than the wealth of this world, called "riches"? Riches and need are set one against the other: yet the

---

2 Eccles. 5:9.
3 Prov. 30:15.
4 Juvenal, *Satires* XIV. 139.

wealth of this world does not remove need but brings it. The smallest portion serves the poor more than great portions please the rich, for "Where there are great riches, there are also many to eat them."[1]

How much the rich can be in need, I myself have often experienced. Thus wealth makes a man not rich, but poor. As one writer puts it,

> He for whom what he has is enough, is surely satisfied.
> He for whom what he has is not enough, is forever in want.
>   Therefore virtue, not wealth, makes plenty;
>   Greed, not poverty, makes need.[2]

IX ·

Exempla Against Covetousness

And oh, how many men covetousness leads astray! How many avarice ruins! An ass refuted Balaam and bruised the foot of the rider because he had a mind to curse Israel, being caught up with the desire of promised rewards. The people stoned Achan because he took gold and silver from the cursed Jericho. Naboth was cut off so that Achab might possess his vineyard. Leprosy struck Giezi because he asked and got silver and clothing in Eliseus' name. Judas hanged himself because he sold Christ. Sudden death wiped out Ananias and Saphira for cheating the Apostle out of the price of a field. "And Tyre has built herself a stronghold and heaped up silver like earth and gold like the mire of the streets. But behold, the Lord shall possess her and shall strike her strength in the sea and she shall be drowned with fire."[1]

---

1 Eccles. 5:10.
2 See Odo of Ceritona in L. Hervieux, *Les fabulistes latins* (Études de Cheriton, 1896), p. 353.
1 Zach. 9:3–4.

X ·

On the Evil Possession of Riches

Therefore it is true, as the wise man asserts, that "Gold and silver have destroyed many."[1] "He who loves gold shall not be justified."[2] Woe to those who strive for it: "Behold these are sinners and yet abounding in the world; they have obtained riches."[3] Hence Truth Himself commanded His apostles, "Do not possess gold nor silver nor money in your purses."[4] Because just as the camel is not able to enter the eye of a needle, so it is difficult for a rich man to enter the kingdom of heaven. For strait is the way and narrow the gate through which one enters that life. The Apostle therefore, following the rule of Truth, said, "Silver and gold I have none."[5] "Woe to you that join house to house and lay field to field, even to the end of the place."[6] "Their land is filled with silver and gold and there is no end to their treasures."[7] "Because of the iniquity of his covetousness, I was angry and I struck him."[8]

XI ·

On Licit Wealth

But was not Abraham rich, Job wealthy, David a man of means? And still the Scripture says of Abraham that "He believed God

1 Ecclus. 8:3.
2 Ecclus. 31:5.
3 Ps. 72:12.
4 Matt. 10:9.
5 Acts 3:6.
6 Isa. 5:8.
7 Isa. 2:7.
8 Isa. 57:17.

and it was reputed to him unto justice,"[1] and of Job that "There is none like him in the earth, a simple and upright man, fearing God and avoiding evil,"[2] and of David that the Lord found him a man after His own heart. But they were "as if having nothing and possessing all things,"[3] according to that saying of the prophet, "If riches abound, set not your heart on them."[4] We, however, possess all things as if having nothing, according to that saying of the psalmist, "The rich have wanted and have suffered hunger."[5]

For you will more easily find a man who loves riches and has them not than you will find one who has them and loves them not; as it is hard to be in fire and not burn, it is harder to have riches and not love them. Hear the prophet: "From the least even to the greatest, all are given to covetousness, and from the prophet even to the priest, all are guilty of deceit."[6]

XII ·

On the Uncertainty of Riches

Every covetous man struggles and strives against nature. For nature brings him into the world poor and takes him out of it poor. The earth received him naked and naked will receive him again. But the covetous man wants to get rich in the world and works to that end. "I will pull down my barns," he says, "and will build bigger ones, and into them I will gather all the things that have come to me and all my goods."[1] But "Thou fool, this night do they require thy soul of thee and whose shall these things be which thou hast provided?"[2] "You store up wealth and you know

1 Gen 15:6.
2 Job 1:8.
3 II Cor. 6:10.
4 Ps. 61:11.
5 Ps. 33:11.
6 Jer. 6:13.
1 Luke 12:18.
2 Luke 12:20.

not for whom you shall gather these things."³ "They have slept their sleep and all the men of riches have found nothing in their hands."⁴ "The rich man when he shall sleep shall take nothing away with him; he shall open his eyes and shall find nothing."⁵

"Be not afraid when a man shall be made rich and when the glory of his house shall be increased; for when he shall die, he shall take nothing away, nor shall his glory go down with him."⁶ But "They shall leave their riches to strangers and their sepulchers shall be their houses forever."⁷ So the wise man gives witness: "He that gathers together by wronging his own soul gathers for others, and another will squander his goods."⁸ And oh, how sad that he who was the enemy then becomes the heir.

XIII ·

On Contempt for the Possession of Riches

Why does anyone bother to acquire things when his own life cannot endure? For "He comes forth like a flower and is destroyed, and he flees like a shadow and never continues in the same state."¹ Why should he want many things when a few suffice? "But having food and clothing," he said, "with these we are content."² Why should he seek necessities with such effort when they turn up without trouble? Hear what Truth says of this. "Do not be solicitous, saying, 'What shall we eat or what shall we drink or what shall we wear?' For your Father knows that you have need of all these things. Seek ye therefore the Kingdom of God and His justice and all these things shall be

3 Ps. 38:7.
4 Ps. 75:6.
5 Job 27:19.
6 Ps. 48:17–18.
7 Ps. 48:11–12.
8 Ecclus. 14:4.
1 Job 14:2.
2 I Tim. 6:8.

added unto you."[3] "I have not seen the just man forsaken nor his seed seeking bread."[4]

XIV ·

On the Avaricious and Covetous Man

Tantalus thirsts amid the waters and the avaricious man is needy in his wealth.[1]

For the avaricious man what he has is the same as what he has not, since he never puts to use what he has but always yearns to acquire more. Solomon says, "One is, as it were, rich when he has nothing, and another is, as it were, poor when he has great riches."[2] The avaricious man, like hell itself, gorges himself without ever being nourished, receives without making a return.

The avaricious man has no pity for those who suffer and no mercy for those who are miserable; but he offends God, his neighbor, and himself. He keeps from God what he owes Him, denies what his neighbor needs, and deprives himself of what is fitting. He is ungrateful to God, uncharitable to his neighbor, and cruel to himself. "Riches are not comely for a covetous and niggardly man, and what should an envious man do with gold?"[3] "He that is evil to himself, to whom will he be good? And he shall not take pleasure in his goods."[4] "He that has the substance of this world and shall see his brother in need and shall close his heart toward him, how does the love of God abide in him?"[5] For he does not love his neighbor as himself: hunger and poverty consume his neighbor! Nor does he love God above all things: for he puts gold and silver above God.

3 Matt. 6:31–33.
4 Ps. 36:25.
1 Horace, *Satires* I. 1. 68.
2 Prov. 13:7.
3 Ecclus. 14:3.
4 Ecclus. 14.5.
5 I John 3:17.

XV ·

Why Avarice Is Called the Service of Idols

The apostle gives a true definition: "Avarice is the service of idols."[1] As the idolator is in servitude to his idol, so the avaricious man is in servitude to his treasure. The idolator devoutly spreads the worship of idols and the avaricious man fondly piles up his hoard of money. The one with all diligence cares for his idol; the other with all solicitude guards his treasure. The one puts his hope in idolatry; the other puts his hope in money. The one fears hurting his idol; the other fears diminishing his treasure.

XVI ·

On the Attributes of the Avaricious

The avaricious man is quick to grasp, slow to give, shameless to refuse. Whatever he spends is a total loss. Sad, querulous, morose, vexed, he sighs, he worries; he clings in doubt to what he has and is unwilling to spend it. He extols a gift but hates to give; he gives only to make a profit, but never makes a profit in order to give. He is free with others' wealth but sparing with his own. He keeps his belly empty to fill his coffer and starves his body to fatten his purse.

"Let not your hand be stretched out to receive and shut when you should give"[1]—closed to giving, open for receiving. For then "the riches of the unjust shall be dried up like a river,"[2] since ill-gotten gains are quickly scattered. It is a sound judgment

1 Col. 3:5.
1 Ecclus. 4:36.
2 Ecclus. 40:13.

that what comes from evil turns to evil, and what comes not from good comes to no good end. Therefore is the avaricious man damned in this life and in the life to come.

XVII ·

Of Gluttony

"The chief thing in the life of a man is water and bread and clothing and a house to cover his shame."[1] And yet the fruits of trees, the different kinds of vegetables, the roots of various plants, the fishes of the sea and beasts of the earth, the birds of the heavens—none of these are enough for the glutton; but he must pick out colors, compare aromas, fatten up plump birds, all of it carefully prepared by gourmet cooks and served in splendor by a staff of butlers and waiters.

One cook mashes and strains, another mixes and churns, and together they turn substance into accident,[2] make nature into art—all this to make satiety become hunger, to awaken an appetite turned squeamish with overeating, to incite gluttony. And their motive is not to sustain nature or supply need, but to bloat up a glutonous craving to eat. And yet the pleasure of gluttony is so short that its span can scarce be measured in minutes.

The glutton scorns moderation and cultivates extravagance. In the diversity of foods and the variety of tastes he knows no measure; his voracity has no bounds. But the result is a heavy stomach, the senses reeling and the mind oppressed; its end is not health but sickness and death. Hear what the wise man says about this: "Be not greedy in any feasting, and do not pour out yourself upon any meat, for in many meats there will be sickness,

1 Ecclus. 29:27. Innocent turns here to his second consideration, the lust of the flesh—i.e., the love of pleasures.

2 A very academic remark, probably ironic; accident is the quality or appearance of things, not essential to their substance or being. Innocent may mean to represent the cooks' efforts as a reversal of the Mass, at which the accidents of bread and wine remained while their substance changed.

and greediness will turn to choler."[3] "Meat for the belly and the belly for the meats, but God will destroy both it and them."[4]

XVIII ·

Exempla Against Gluttony

Gluttony demands a heavy tribute but gives the meanest returns: the more delicate the food, the more stinking the dung. What was foul to swallow comes out fouler, making vile gases above and below and hideous noises. Gluttony it was that closed paradise, sold our birthright, hanged the chef, beheaded the Baptist. For Nabuzardan, the head chef, burned the temple and demolished all Jerusalem; at a banquet Balthasar saw the handwriting on the wall, "Mane, Thecel, Phares," and in the same night was killed by the Chaldeans. "The people sat down to eat and to drink and they rose up to play;"[1] but "the food was still in their mouth when the wrath of God came upon them."[2] "They who have fed delicately have died in the streets."[3] And Dives, who feasted in splendor every day, lies buried in hell.

XIX ·

On Drunkenness

Or what is more shameful than a drunkard?—whose breath stinks, whose body trembles; who says silly things and gives away secrets; who loses his reason and distorts his face. "There is no secret where drunkenness reigns."[1]

3 Ecclus. 37:32–33.
4 I Cor. 6:13.
1 I Cor. 10:7.
2 Ps. 77:30–31.
3 Lam. 4:5.
1 Prov. 31:4.

Whom has the flowing bowl not made talkative?[2]

For then wine is not enough, nor ale, nor beer; but they must make mead, heavy wine and light wine with much labor and care and at no small expense. And from these arise disputes and quarrels, then fights and brawls. As the wise man says, "Wine drunken to excess raises quarrels and wrath and many ruins."[3] And Osee says, "Fornication and wine and drunkenness take away the understanding."[4] Wherefore the Apostle says, "Do not be drunk with wine in which there is luxury."[5] And Solomon says, "Wine is a luxurious thing and drunkenness is riotous."[6] The sons of Rechab and the son of Zachary did not drink wine nor beer nor anything which could make one drunk.

XX ·

Exempla Against Drunkenness

Drunkenness bared Noah's private parts, committed incest, killed the king's son, and cut the throat of the commander-in-chief. Therefore what Solomon says is true: "They who give themselves to drinking and who club together shall be consumed."[1] And Isaiah, "Woe to you who rise up early in the morning to follow drunkenness and to drink until the evening so that you are inflamed with wine. The harp and the lyre and the timbrel and the pipe and wine are in your feasts."[2] "Woe to you that are mighty to drink wine and stout men at drunkenness!"[3] "Behold joy and gladness, killing calves and slaying rams, eating flesh and drinking wine: Let us eat and drink for tomorrow we die. And

2 Horace, *Epistles* I. v. 19.
3 Ecclus. 31:38.
4 Osee 4:11.
5 Cf. Eph. 5:18.
6 Prov. 20:1.

1 Prov. 23:21.
2 Isa. 5:11–12.
3 Isa. 5:22.

the voice of the Lord of Hosts was revealed in my ears: Surely this iniquity will not be forgiven you until you die."[4] Woe to Ephraim's crown of pride. The priest and the prophet were ignorant; through drunkenness they were soaked up in wine; they knew not him who sees; they were ignorant of judgment. For shame! When the blessing was asked of a certain Father Superior at the beginning of the daily reading from the Gospel, it is said that, belching from the drunkenness of the day and night before, he said with a loud voice, "May the King of the Angels bless the drink of His servants."[5]

XXI ·

On Lust

A shameless mother will bring forth a more shameless daughter. This is justly said: "He that is filthy, let him be filthy still."[1] "They are all adulterers, like an oven heated by a baker. The princes began to be mad with wine:"[2]

> Fill their bellies up with wine,
> On Venus' couch men fast recline.[3]

O extreme shame of lust, which not only makes the mind effeminate but weakens the body; not only stains the soul but fouls the person. "Every sin that a man commits is outside his body, but he that commits fornication sins against his own body."[4]

Always, hot desire and wantonness precede lust, stench and

[4] Isa. 22:13–14.

[5] See the Table Blessings in the monastic Breviary: "May Christ, the King of the Angels, bless the food of His servants." The story was probably a commonplace joke among clerics.

[1] Apoc. 22:11.

[2] Osee 7:4–5.

[3] Source unknown.

[4] I Cor. 6:18.

filth accompany it, sorrow and repentance follow it. "The lips
of the harlot are like a dripping honeycomb and her throat
smoother than oil; but her end is as bitter as wormwood and her
tongue is as sharp as a two-edged sword."[5]

XXII ·

On the Universality of Lust

The enemy is one of your own household, living not far off
but near, not outside but within; for "his strength is in his
loins and his force in the navel on his belly."[1] Lust is never put
to flight except by flight, and never mortified except by torment.
It needs freedom and abundance as its cause; but for its effect it
invents its own means and opportunities. This vice corrupts
every age, disturbs either sex, breaks all order, undermines each
class of society. For it assaults both young and old, men and
women, wise and foolish, higher and lower; and last, even
priests, who embrace Venus at night and then worship the Virgin
at dawn. It is shameful to speak of this and the more shameful to
do it, but let it be said in hopes that speaking out will discourage
the practice: At night they excite the son of Venus on a bed, at
dawn they offer the Son of the Virgin on an altar.

XXIII ·

On the Various Kinds of Lust

Who could untangle well enough the many kinds of lust? For
this destroyed the Five Cities with the neighboring region;
ruined Sichem and its people; struck down Her and Onan, sons
of Juda; pierced both the Jew and the Medianite woman with

5 Prov. 5:3-4.
1 Job 40:11.

a dagger; destroyed the tribe of Benjamin for the wife of a Levite; felled in war the sons of Eli the priest; killed Urias, murdered Ammon, stoned the elders, cursed Ruben, seduced Samson, and perverted Solomon.

Hence the statement is true which reads, "Many have perished by the beauty of a woman."[1] For "Wine and women make wise men fall off, and shall rebuke the prudent."[2] "She has cast down many wounded, and the strongest have been slain by her. Her house is the road to hell, reaching even to the inner chambers of death."[3] She weakens the strong, blurs the senses, wastes time, and squanders wealth.

XXIV ·

On Unnatural Intercourse

This vice causes an ignominious change, which the Apostle feared not to name: "For this cause God delivered them up to shameful lusts. For their women have changed the natural use into that use which is against nature. And in like manner the men also, leaving the natural use of the women, have burned in their lusts, one towards another: men with men, working that which is filthy."[1] What is more shameful than such shamefulness? what more criminal than these crimes? In the Law, intercourse of a man with a man is treated as equal to intercourse between a man and a beast. So one reads in Leviticus: "Thou shalt not lie with mankind as with womankind because it is an abomination. Thou shalt not copulate with any beast, nor be defiled with it."[2] For each of these the same penalty is prescribed: "If anyone lie with a man as with a woman, both have committed an abomination; let them be put to death; the beast also you shall kill."[3] He who

1 Ecclus. 9:9.
2 Ecclus. 19:2.
3 Prov. 7:26–27.

1 Rom. 1:26–27.
2 Lev. 18:22–23.
3 Lev. 20:13, 15.

has ears to hear, let him hear; and he who has acted foolishly, let him come to his senses.

XXV ·

On the Punishment of This Crime

The penalty this crime deserved taught a lesson: "The Lord rained brimstone and fire from heaven on Sodom and Gomorrha."[1] God did not wish to give the execution of this punishment to any angel or man; according to Scripture, he reserved the vengeance for such crimes to Himself: "Revenge is mine, and I will repay them."[2] Therefore the Lord rained out of Himself not rain and dew, but brimstone and fire: brimstone for the stench of lust, fire for the heat of passion—a penalty fit for the crime. Nor does it say He "sent," but He "rained," so that the very word emphasizes the magnitude and extent of the penalty. His eye spared no one; He destroyed them all at once. The wife of Lot, who looked back, He changed into a pillar of salt; and not only the cities but all the surrounding region He changed into a Dead Sea and a valley of salt. "It is a fearful thing to fall into the hands of the living God,"[3] who shows in great measure patience of His mercy, but inflicts the vengeance of His justice with equal severity.

XXVI ·

Of the Ambitious Man

Thus while the avaricious gather wealth and misers save it, while gluttons swallow their pleasures and lechers wallow in theirs, the ambitious strive for honors and the proud esteem them.[1] The

1 Gen. 19:24.
2 Deut. 32:35.
3 Heb. 10:31.

1 Innocent turns here to his third consideration, the pride of life—i.e., the love of honors.

ambitious man is always fearful, always under tension lest he say or do anything which might make him displeasing in the eyes of men. He pretends humility, feigns honesty, displays affability, shows off his kindness, is accommodating, is compliant, honors everyone and bows to everybody, frequents courts, visits important people, rises and embraces, claps his hands and fawns. A famous quotation describes him well:

If there's no dust, he'll still brush it off.[2]

He is prompt and eager where he knows he will please, hesitant and lukewarm where he thinks he will not. He condemns evil and detests iniquity, but what he praises and blames varies with the person, so long as he will be thought competent and be deemed welcome, be praised and approved by one and all. But see how he must keep up a grave battle in himself, and a very hard conflict it is, with Iniquity hammering at his soul and Ambition leading him by the hand; for what the one suggests he do, the other will not permit. And yet Iniquity and Ambition, mother and daughter, plot for one another: the mother lives in the open and the daughter, kept in hiding, never resists—one claims a public and the other a secret domain.

The ambitious man is only too happy to seek the public office he desires, saying, "O when will a man hold high office who is severe in justice, dutiful in mercy, who is not drawn aside by love or hate, not corrupted by pleas or bribes, who believes in the faithful and yields to the suppliant, is humble and kind, generous, mild, constant, patient, wise and astute?"

XXVII •

On the Excessive Desires of the Ambitious Man

If he does not profit by one device, he moves to another. He

2 Ovid, *Ars amatoria* I. 151.

calls upon Simon and then turns to Giezi; through him he strives to buy what he cannot obtain by himself; he begs and promises, makes offers and pays commissions. For shame! By right or wrong he strives to get the favor he could not get gratis. Nor does he stop at that, but pursues honor and tries to take it by violence, snatches impudently at rank—why, he is set aflame by the support of friends, the assistance of neighbors, by such a flame of hell, such a lust to be first, that he does not abhor schism nor fear scandal. But leprosy struck Giezi down, Simon died with his money, fire consumed Core and his accomplices, and the earth swallowed Dathan and Abiron alive. Let no one assume any honor but him who is called by God, as Aaron was.

XXVIII ·

An Exemplum of Ambition

A clear exemplum of ambition is found in Absalom, who, when he aspired to be king, "made himself chariots and horsemen and fifty men to run before him. And Absalom rising up early stood by the entrance of the gate; and when any man had business to come to the king's judgment, Absalom called him to him and said, 'Of what city art thou?' He answered and said, 'Thy servant is of such a tribe of Israel.' And Absalom answered him, 'Thy words seem to me good and just. But there is no man appointed by the king to hear thee.' And Absalom said, 'O that they would make me judge over the land, that all that have business might come to me that I might do them justice.' Moreover, when any man came to him to salute him, he put forth his hand and took him and kissed him. And this he did to all Israel that came for judgment, to be heard by the king; and he enticed the hearts of the men of Israel."[1] And when Absalom had gone to Hebron, "He sent spies into all the tribes of Israel, saying, 'As

[1] II Kings 15:1–6.

soon as you shall hear the sound of the trumpet, say ye, "Absalom reigneth in Hebron." ' "[2] And "There was a strong conspiracy, and the people running together increased with Absalom."[3]

XXIX ·

That the Life of Great Men Is Short and Miserable

But suppose a man is lifted up high, suppose he is raised to the very peak. At once his cares grow heavy, his worries mount up, he eats less and cannot sleep. And so nature is corrupted, his spirit weakened, his sleep disturbed, his appetite lost; his strength is diminished, he loses weight. Exhausting himself, he scarcely lives half a lifetime and ends his wretched days with a more wretched death.

This poetic saying is true:

> Great structures collapse upon themselves,
>   and the highest ones cannot stand long:
> They are raised up on high
> Only to fall the harder.[1]

But this prophetic saying is even truer: "I have seen the wicked highly exalted and lifted up like the cedars of Lebanon. And I passed by, and lo, he was not; and I sought him and his place was not found."[2] Before his days are full he shall perish, he shall be blasted even as will the vineyard when its grapes are in first flower, and the olive tree when it puts forth its blossoms. Hear what the wise man says: "All power is of a short life."[3]

[2] II Kings 15:10.
[3] II Kings 15:12.
[1] Claudian, *In Rufinam I.* 22–23; Lucan, *Belli Civilis.* 1. 81; 70–71.
[2] Ps. 36:35–36.
[3] Ecclus. 10:11.

XXX ·

On the Various Attributes of the Proud

And yet as soon as the ambitious man is promoted to an honor, he becomes puffed up with pride and unrestrained in boasting; he does not care to be serviceable, for he glories in being ahead. And as he sees himself above others, he presumes he is better. Yet it is not rank but virtue that makes a man good; not office but character. A proud man disdains his former friends, ignores acquaintances made yesterday, is contemptuous to old companions. He turns his head, raises his eyes, stiffens his neck, assumes a haughty look; then he begins to speak of grand matters and have big ideas. He cannot stand being subordinate, strives to be ahead; he is hostile to his superiors, overbearing to his inferiors. He will not put up with annoyances or put off any plans; he is rash and bold, pretentious and arrogant, pompous and churlish.

XXXI ·

On the Pride and Fall of Lucifer

Pride, unbearable and hateful to everyone, among all vices you are forever first and last: every sin is committed when you appear, and every sin renounced when you depart. For it is written, "The beginning of every sin is pride,"[1] "the first born of death."[2] Pride at the very beginning of creation lifted up the creature against the Creator, the angel against God. But without delay it threw him down, because he stood not in the truth; from inno-

---

[1] Ecclus. 10:15.
[2] Job 18:13.

cence into sin, from delights into miseries, from empyrean heaven into caliginous space.

Hear now the prophet: "How art thou fallen from heaven, O Lucifer, who didst rise in the morning? And thou saidst in thy heart, 'I will ascend into heaven. I will exalt my throne above the stars of God. I will sit in the mountain of the covenant, in the sides of the north. I will ascend above the height of the clouds. I will be like the most High.'"[3] "Thou wast the seal of resemblance, full of wisdom and perfect in beauty. Thou wast in the pleasures of the paradise of God; every precious stone was thy covering: the sardius, the topaz and the jasper, the chrysolite and the onyx and the beryl, the sapphire and the carbuncle and the emerald: gold the work of thy beauty, and thy pipes were prepared in the day that thou wast created. Thou, a cherub stretched out and protecting, and I set thee in the holy mountain of God; thou hast walked in the midst of the stones of fire. Thou wast perfect in thy ways from the day of thy creation until iniquity was found in thee. Thou hast sinned, and I cast thee out from the mountain of God. Thy heart was lifted up with thy beauty, and I have cast thee to the ground."[4] "The cedars in the paradise of God were not higher than he; the fir trees did not equal his top; neither were the plane trees to be compared with him for branches. No precious tree in the paradise of God was like him in his beauty. For I made him beautiful and thick set with many branches."[5] "He is king over all the children of pride."[6] He is "a great red dragon, having seven heads and ten horns and on his heads seven diadems. And his tail drew the third part of the stars of heaven and cast them to the earth."[7] "And that great dragon was cast out, that old serpent, who is called the devil and Satan, who seduces the whole world. And he was cast unto the earth, and his angels were thrown down with him."[8] And of this it is

3 Isa. 14:12–14.
4 Ezech. 28:12–17.
5 Ezech. 31:8–9.
6 Job 41:25.
7 Apoc. 12:3–4.
8 Apoc. 12:9.

said truly, "I saw Satan like lightning falling from heaven."[9] For "Everyone who exalts himself shall be humbled and he who humbles himself shall be exalted."[10]

XXXII ·

On the Arrogance of Man

O proud presumption, O presumptuous pride, which not only wished to make angels equal to God, but presumed to make men into God. Then did it pull down those it had lifted up, and made humble those it had exalted. Wherefore our Lord said through the mouth of the prophet, "Son of man, say to the prince of Tyre, 'Thus saith the Lord God: Because thy heart is lifted up as the heart of God and thou hast said, "I am God," whereas thou art a man and not God, I will bring upon thee the strongest of the nations; they shall kill thee and thou shalt die the death of them that are slain.' "[1]

Nebuchadnezzar proudly boasted of his power, saying "Is not this the great Babylon which I have built to be the seat of the kingdom, by the strength of my power and in the glory of my excellence? And while the word was yet in the king's mouth, a voice came down from heaven: 'To thee, O king Nebuchadnezzar, it is said, Thy kingdom shall pass from thee, and they shall cast thee out from among men; and thy dwelling shall be with cattle and wild beasts. Thou shalt eat grass like an ox, and seven times shall pass over thee till thou know that the most High ruleth in the kingdom of men and giveth it to whomsoever He will.' The same hour the word was fulfilled upon Nebuchadnezzar."[2] And therefore it is true, as we read in the Holy Scripture,

9 Luke 10:18.
10 Luke 14:11.
1 Ezech. 28:2, 6-8.
2 Dan. 4:27-30.

"And man when he was in honor did not understand; he is compared to senseless beasts and is become like to them."[3]

Pride overthrew the tower of Babel and confounded language; it brought Goliath low and hanged Aman, killed Nicanor, ruined Antiochus, drowned Pharaoh, slew Sennacherib. God pulls down the seats of proud princes, and dries up the roots of proud nations.

XXXIII ·

On the Abomination of Pride

How detestable pride is, our Lord Himself bears witness through the mouth of the prophet: "The Lord God hath sworn by his own soul, saith the Lord, the God of hosts: I detest the pride of Jacob."[1] And "The Lord hath sworn against the pride of Jacob: Surely I will never forget all their works."[2] Wherefore among those six things which the Lord hates, plus the seventh which His soul detests, Solomon places first the haughty eye, which is to say, pride.

And Isaiah says, "The day of the Lord of hosts shall be upon everyone that is proud and highminded, and upon everyone that is arrogant, and he shall be humbled. And upon all the tall and lofty cedars of Lebanon, and upon all the oaks of Bashan, and upon all the high mountains, and upon all the elevated hills, and upon every high tower, and every fenced wall, and the loftiness of men shall be bowed down, and the haughtiness of men shall be humbled."[3] "Therefore hath hell enlarged her soul and opened her mouth without any bounds; and their strong ones and their people and their high and glorious ones shall go down into it."[4] "The Lord of hosts hath designed it, to pull down the

3 Ps. 48:13.
1 Amos 6:8.
2 Amos 8:7.
3 Isa. 2:12–15, 17.
4 Isa. 5:14.

pride of all glory."[5] Hear also what Job says, "If his pride mount up even to heaven, and his head touch the clouds, in the end he shall be destroyed like a dunghill."[6]

XXXIV ·

Against the Arrogance of the Proud

Almost every evil man loves anyone who is like himself, but the proud man hates anyone who is exalted. Whence Solomon says, "Among the proud there are always contentions,"[1] and "Where pride is, there also shall be reproach."[2] The proud man is eager for anything unusual, hating anything ordinary. He considers it a great thing if he deigns to speak to someone, and the grandest thing in the world if he rises or pays respects to someone. He thinks that his honorable position has gained more from him than he from it. Never does he have any use for power gained from ancestors. But his pride, his arrogance, and his disdain are greater than his strength of character.

Let him turn over in his mind what we read in the Holy Gospel: "And there was also a strife among the disciples of Jesus, which of them should seem to be the greater. And Jesus said to them, 'The kings of the Gentiles lord it over them; and they that have power over them are called beneficent. But you not so; but he that is the greater among you, let him become as the younger, and he that is the leader as he that serves.' "[3] And Peter, the head of the apostles: "Neither as lording it over the clergy, but being made a pattern of the flock from the heart."[4]

"The earth is the Lord's and the fulness thereof, the world and

5 Isa. 23:9.
6 Job 20:6–7.
1 Prov. 13:10.
2 Prov. 11:2.
3 Luke 22:24–26.
4 I Pet. 5:3.

all they that dwell therein."[5] Wherefore there is one God and one Lord; others are not lords but servants; lordship is prohibited to them, and they are told to serve. Hear the words of the wise man on this point: "Have they made thee ruler? Be not lifted up; be among them as one of them."[6]

XXXV ·

Against the Deceit of Ambitious Men

The sons of Zebadee, through their mother's intervention, asked an honor from Christ: "Say that these my two sons may sit, the one on thy right hand and the other on thy left, in thy kingdom."[1] Here was the answer they deserved: "You know not what you ask."[2] For it is not through honors but through onerous service that one arrives at the Kingdom. Whence the Lord added, "It is not mine to give to you."[3] Certainly it is His to give, but not to you, ambitious men that you are. All power, it is true, comes from God, but the proud man does not rule through God —as thus in the prophet's formulary: "They have reigned, but not by me; they have been princes, and I knew it not."[4]

XXXVI ·

On the Qualities of the Arrogant

The proud man "loves the first places at feasts and the first chairs in the synagogues, and salutations in the market place,

[5] Ps. 23:1.
[6] Ecclus. 32:1.
[1] Matt. 20:21.
[2] Matt. 20:22.
[3] Matt. 20:23.
[4] Osee 8:4.

and to be called by men, Rabbi."[1] He does not wish to be called by his own name, but by the name of his position. He wishes to be honored not as a man, but as God. He seats himself over the heads of others, he struts about, he expects everyone to rise in his presence and bow to him.

Once a certain philosopher, wishing to ridicule the arrogance of a certain king, when he saw him sitting up high on the royal throne, fell down on the earth and worshipped him in suppliant wise. And then all of a sudden without invitation he went up and sat beside the king. The king was amazed, and knowing that the man was a philosopher demanded the reason why he had done this. Whereupon the philosopher replied, "Either you are God or you are a man; if God, I must worship you; if a man, I may sit beside you." But the king, turning the philosopher's answer against him, retorted, "But then, if I am a man, you must not worship me; if God, you must not sit beside me." The philosopher replied wisely, but the king cleverly outmaneuvered him.

XXXVII ·

On Superfluous Adornment

God made girdles for our first parents after their sin, and Christ says to Christians, "Do not have two coats."[1] Also according to the counsel of John, "He who has two coats should give to him who has none."[2] But the proud man, so that he may seem magnificent, goes out of his way to be clothed with more than one garment, of soft materials adorned with costly things. And yet what is a man adorned with gems but a whited sepulcher outside and full of rottenness within? Blue and purple cloth, scarlet and fine linen rot in the ground; gold and silver, precious stones and

1 Matt 23:6–7.
1 Luke 9:3.
2 Luke 3:11.

gems tarnish and grow dull in the mire. Dignity and power lie uneasy in the dust, honor and glory seem strange amid the ashes.

Why then, O proud man, do you widen your phylacteries and enlarge your tassels? For Dives, clothed in purple and fine linen, lies buried in hell. According to Josephus,[3] Dina, daughter of the patriarch Jacob, remained a virgin until she went out to buy an ornament from the women of the country; but when she went out, Sichem, son of the king of Hemor, raped her. Holofernes sat in a tent woven of purple and cloth of gold, adorned with emeralds and precious stones; his head was cut off by Judith, who had before worn a hair-shirt but then wore the garments of joy.

Hear the opinion of the wise man on this point: "Glory not in apparel at any time."[4] And the Apostle adds, "Not in costly attire,"[5] "not in the outward plaiting of the hair, or the wearing of gold, or the putting on of apparel."[6]

XXXVIII ·

Against Superfluous Adornment

Hear what our Lord threatens, through the mouth of the prophet, against superfluous adornments: "Because the daughters of Sion are haughty and have walked with stretched out necks and wanton glances of their eyes, the Lord will make bald the crown of the head of the daughters of Sion; and the Lord will discover their hair. In that day the Lord will take away the ornaments of shoes, and little moons, and chains, and necklaces, and bracelets, and bonnets, and bodkins, and ornaments of the legs, and tablets, and sweet balls, and earrings, and rings, and jewels hanging on the forehead, and changes of ap-

---

[3] Josephus, *Antiquitates Judaicae* I. 21. 1.
[4] Ecclus. 11:4.
[5] I Tim. 2:9.
[6] I Pet. 3:3.

parel, and short cloaks, and fine linen, and crisping pins, and looking-glasses, and lawns, and headbands, and fine veils. And instead of a sweet smell there shall be stench, and instead of a girdle a cord, and instead of curled hair, baldness, and instead of a stomacher, haircloth."[1]

And lo, a just punishment will be meted out for this guilt, so that they will be struck down where they have sinned. And hear yet still another prophet speaking on this subject: "O Tyre, fine embroidered linen from Egypt was woven for thy sail, to be spread on thy mast; blue and purple from the islands of Elisa were made thy covering. They exchanged for thy price teeth of ivory and ebony. They set forth precious stones and purple and embroidered works and fine linen and silk and chodchod in thy market. The men of Dedan were thy merchants for tapestry for seats, and thou wast replenished and glorified exceedingly. Now thou art destroyed by the sea; thy riches are at the bottom of the waters; thou art brought to nothing, and thou shalt never be any more."[2]

XXXIX ·

That More Honor Is Given to Clothing than to Virtue

A certain philosopher, wearing mean clothing, came to the palace of a prince and, after knocking, was not admitted for a long time. As often as he tried to enter, as often was he repelled. Then he changed his clothes, adorning himself; at his first cry the door was opened to him. Proceeding to the feet of the prince, he began reverently to kiss the prince's cloak. The prince was amazed at this, and demanded the reason why he had done it. The philosopher replied, "I honor what confers honor; what

1 Isa. 3:16–24.
2 Ezech. 27:7, 15–16, 20, 25, 34, 36.

my virtue was incapable of, my clothing obtained for me." "O
vanity of vanities,"[1] more honor is given to clothing than to virtue, more honor to charm than to righteousness.

XL ·

*On Adornment of the Person, Table,
and House*

An artificial countenance is plastered on, the natural face
covered up, as if man's skill could surpass the art of his Creator.
Not so, not so. For He said, "Consider the lilies of the field; they
grow and neither toil nor spin. Yet I say to you that not even
Solomon in all his glory was arrayed like one of these."[1] But far
be it that a counterfeit color be compared with natural color;
indeed, when the face is painted it takes on an abominable
stench. "All things are vanity, every man living."[2] For what is
more vain than to comb the locks, paint the face, smooth the
hair on the head, rouge the cheeks, elongate the eyebrows, when
"Favor is deceitful and beauty is vain."[3] "All flesh is grass, and
all the glory thereof as the flower of the field,"[4] because "They
shall shortly wither away as grass, and as the green herbs shall
quickly fall."[5]

But let me pass over personal adornments lest I seem more
evil-minded than truthful, out of personal rancor. What then is
more vain than to decorate a table with pictured cloths, ivory-
handled knives, gold vases and silver vessels, goblets and cups,
platters and dishes, salvers and spoons, forks and salt-cellers,
basins and pitchers, boxes and fans?

1 Eccles. 1:2.
1 Matt. 6:28–29.
2 Ps. 38:6.
3 Prov. 31:30.
4 Isa. 40:6.
5 Ps. 36:2.

What good does it do to paint chambers and embellish porches, decorate an entrance, cover a floor, stuff a bed with feathers and cover it with silks, enclosing it with a curtain or canopy? For it is written: "When he shall die, he shall take nothing away; nor shall his glory descend with him."[6]

End of Book Two

6 Ps. 48:18.

BOOK THREE: The Damnable Exit from the Human Condition

I ·

On the Damnable Exit from the Human
Condition

No one can boast of the cleanness of his heart, since "in many things we all offend."[1] "And if we say that we have no sin, we deceive ourselves and the truth is not in us."[2] Who can say, as the Apostle did, "I am not conscious to myself of anything, yet am I not hereby justified."[3] "Who is this man and we will praise him?"[4] "Behold among his saints none is unchangeable, and the heavens are not pure in his sight,"[5] "and in his angels he found wickedness."[6] "How much more is man abominable and unprofitable who drinks iniquity like water?"[7]

"And God repented that He had made man on the earth, seeing that the wickedness of men was great upon the earth and that all the thought of their heart was bent upon evil at all times, and so being touched inwardly with sorrow of heart, he destroyed man whom he had created."[8] For sure iniquity has abounded and charity grown cold. "All have gone astray and

1 Jas. 3:2.
2 I John 1:8.
3 I Cor. 4:4.
4 Ecclus. 31:9.
5 Job 15:15.
6 Job 4:18.
7 Job 15:16.
8 Gen. 6:5-7.

have become unprofitable; there is none who does good, no, not even one."[9]

Almost the whole life of mortals is full of mortal sin, so that one can scarcely find anyone who does not go astray, does not return to his own vomit and rot in his own dung. Instead they "are glad when they have done evil and rejoice in most wicked things."[10] "Being filled with all iniquity, malice, fornication, avarice, wickedness, full of envy, murders, contention, deceit, evil, being whisperers, detractors, hateful to God, irreverent, proud, haughty, plotters of evil, disobedient to parents, foolish, dissolute, without affection, without fidelity, without mercy."[11] This world is full of such and worse; it abounds in heretics and schismatics, traitors and tyrants, simonists and hypocrites; the ambitious and the covetous, robbers and brigands, violent men, extortionists, usurers, forgers; the impious and sacrilegious, the betrayers and liars, the flatterers and deceivers; gossips, tricksters, gluttons, drunkards; adulterers, incestuous men, deviates, and the dirty-minded; the lazy, the careless, the vain, the prodigal, the impetuous, the irascible, the impatient and inconstant; poisoners, fortune tellers, perjurers, cursers; men who are presumptuous and arrogant, unbelieving and desperate; and finally those ensnared in all vices together. Indeed, "As smoke vanishes and as wax melts before the fire, so let the wicked perish at the presence of God."[12]

II ·

On the Agonies Which the Wicked Experience in Death

The wicked suffer four agonies in death. The first is bodily pain, of such greatness and severity as never is or has been in this pres-

9 Ps. 13:3.
10 Prov. 2:14.
11 Rom. 1:29–31.
12 Ps. 67:3.

ent life before its end. In some cases, though not in all, it appears that excessive pain makes them tear themselves to pieces. For a strong and incomparable violence arises when the ties between body and soul burst asunder. Whence the prophet says in his lamentation, "The sorrows of death have encompassed me."[1] Note how he says "have encompassed me." There is not a member or joint in the body which is not deeply involved in that inexplicable pain.

The second pain occurs when the body, fully wearied, has exhausted its strength: then the soul sees far more vividly in a flash all its good and bad deeds projected before its inner eye. This pain is so great and the revulsion from it so severe because the soul in its deepest perturbation is forced almost to hate itself. Whence it is said, "The torrents of iniquity troubled me."[2] Those torrents come with enormous force and seem to destroy all, so that in the moment of death the evil man sees all his deeds, good and bad, flash before his eyes.

The third pain occurs when the soul already begins to judge itself with justice, and sees each act in its own iniquity and the due torments of hell threatening. Whence it is said, "The sorrows of death have encompassed me, etc."[3]

The fourth pain occurs when the soul, still in the body, sees evil spirits ready to drag it off; at this point the pain and fear are so great that the miserable soul, however lost, holds back as long as it can and would ransom the time of its captivity before it leaves the body.

III ·

On the Coming of Christ on the Day of Any Man's Death

Before their souls leave their bodies, good and evil alike will see Christ upon the Cross. The evil will see Him to their confusion:

1 Ps. 114:3.
2 Ps. 17:5.
3 Ps. 114:3.

they will blush with shame, being through their own fault unre-
deemed by the blood of Christ. Whence it is said of the evil,
"They will look upon him whom they have pierced,"[1] which
signifies His coming on judgment day and also on the day of
each man's death. But the good will see Him to their joy. And
this we know from the words of the Apostle, "Until the day of
the coming of our Lord Jesus Christ,"[2] that is, until the day of
death when Christ on the Cross will appear to the good and evil
alike. And Christ Himself said of John the Evangelist, "So I
will have him to remain until I come";[3] that is, persevering in
virginity until I come at his death.

We read about four comings of Christ. Two are visible: the
first in the flesh, the second at judgment. And two are invisible:
the first in the soul through grace, whence "We will come to him
and will make our abode with him";[4] and the second at the death
of each of the faithful, whence John says, "Come, Lord Jesus."[5]
Wherefore death is called a meeting, because Christ comes to
meet the soul.

IV ·

On the Putrefaction of the Dead Body

"His spirit shall go forth, and he shall return into his earth; in
that day all their thoughts shall perish."[1] O how many great
plans mortals make for the uncertain future of this world! but at
the moment of sudden death, their plans suddenly vanish. "I
am taken away like a shadow when it declines, and I am shaken
off like locusts."[2] So the spirit does not go forth voluntarily, but

1 John 19:37.
2 I Cor. 1:8.
3 John 21:22.
4 John 14:23.
5 Apoc. 22:20.

1 Ps. 145:4.
2 Ps. 108:23.

unwillingly: it loses with sorrow what it possessed with love, and willy-nilly it has a limit which it cannot pass when earth must return to earth. For it is written, "Earth thou art, and unto earth thou shalt return."[3]

For it is natural that what is made of matter should return to matter. "He shall take away their breath and they shall fail and shall return to their dust."[4] But when man shall die, his heirs will be beasts, serpents, and worms. "For they shall all sleep in the dust, and worms shall cover them."[5] "For the worm shall eat them up as a garment and the moth shall consume them as wool."[6] "I am to be consumed as rottenness, and as a garment that is moth-eaten."[7] "I have said to rottenness, 'Thou art my father'; to worms, 'my mother and my sister'."[8] "Man is rottenness, and the son of a man is a worm."[9] O vile father, ghastly mother, abominable sister! Man is conceived of blood made rotten by the heat of lust; and in the end worms, like mourners, stand about his corpse. In life he produced lice and tapeworms; in death he will produce worms and flies. In life he produced dung and vomit; in death he produces rottenness and stench. In life he fattened one man; in death he fattens a multitude of worms. What then is more foul than a human corpse? What is more horrible than a dead man? He whose embrace was pure delight in life will be a gruesome sight in death.

Of what advantage, then, are riches, food, and honors? For riches will not free us from death, neither food protect us from the worm nor honors from the stench. That man who but now sat in glory upon a throne is now looked down on in the grave; the dandy who once glittered in his palace lies now naked and vile in his tomb; and he who supped once on delicacies in his hall is now in his sepulcher food for worms.

---

3 Gen. 3:19.
4 Ps. 103:29.
5 Job 21:26.
6 Isa. 51:8.
7 Job 13:28.
8 Job 17:14.
9 Job 25:6.

V ·

On the Sad Memories of the Damned

"The vengeance on the flesh of the ungodly is worm and fire."[1] Double for both: a worm and fire inside him which gnaws and burns the heart, and an exterior worm and fire which gnaws and burns the body. "Their worm," he says, "shall not die, and their fire shall not be quenched."[2] "The Lord shall put fire and worms in their flesh so that they will burn and feel it forever."[3] The worm of conscience will destroy them in these three ways: it will trouble them with memories, disturb them with repentance, and torture them with anguish. "They shall come with fear at the thought of their crimes, and their iniquities shall stand against them to convict them,"[4] saying, "What has pride profited us? or what advantage has the boasting of riches brought us? All those things are passed away like a shadow, and like a ship that passes through the waves whose trace cannot be found when it is gone by."[5] So also with us: as soon as we are born we start ceasing to be, and we can show no sign of virtue but are consumed in our own iniquity. With boundless perturbation they recall what they had done in their lives with excessive delight: the prick of memory pierces them in punishment, as the very goad of their wickedness had incited them to sin.

VI ·

On the Useless Repentance of the Damned

And they will say to themselves, repenting, "We have erred

---

[1] Ecclus. 7:19. Innocent turns here to a second subtopic, hell and damnation.

[2] Isa. 66:24.

[3] Judith 16:21.

[4] Wisd. 4:20.

[5] Wisd. 5:8–10.

from the way of truth and the light of justice has not shined on us."[1] "Then they will begin to say to the mountains, 'Fall upon us,' and to the hills, 'Cover us'."[2] They will repent in their punishment, but not be restored to God's favor. It is just that those who would not repent when they could, cannot repent when they would, for God gave them their time to repent and they abused it.

On this account the rich man who was tortured in the flame said to Abraham, " 'Father, I beseech you to send Lazarus to my father's house, for I have five brothers, so that he may testify to them, lest they also come into this place of torments.' When Abraham said to him, 'They have Moses and the prophets, let them hear them,' he replied, 'No, Father Abraham, but if one went to them from the dead, they will do penance'."[3] That man was doing penance in hell, but because he knew it was fruitless, he asked that his brothers be told, that they might do some fruitful penance in this world; for it profits a man to repent when he is still able to sin.

VII ·

On the Unspeakable Anguish of the Damned

"Seeing it, they shall be troubled with a terrible fear, groaning from anguish of spirit and saying, 'These are they whom we had sometime in derision and for a parable of reproach; we fools esteemed their life madness and their end without honor. Behold how they are numbered among the children of God, and their lot is among the saints'."[1]

One punishment of the wicked will be to contemplate the glory of the saints, though perhaps after the final judgment. The saints shall behold the damned in torment, according to this

1 Wisd. 5:6.
2 Luke 23:30.
3 Luke 16:27–30.
1 Wisd. 5:2–5.

text: "The just shall rejoice when he shall see the revenge on the wicked."[2] But the wicked will not behold the saints in glory, according to this text: "Let the wicked be taken away, lest he might see the glory of God."[3] Sinners in hell will say such things as this because "the hope of the wicked is as dust which is blown away with the wind, and as a thin froth which is dispersed by the storm, and as a smoke which is scattered abroad by the wind, and as a memory of a guest of one day."[4]

VIII ·

On the Various Punishments of Hell

There are various punishments in hell for various kinds of sin. The first punishment is fire, the second cold. Of these the Lord says, "There will be weeping and gnashing of teeth,"[1] weeping because of the smoke, gnashing of teeth because of the cold. The third punishment will be stench. Of these three it is said, "Fire and brimstone and storms of winds shall be the portion of their cup."[2] The fourth is the never-failing worm, of which it is said, "Their worm shall not die and their fire shall not be quenched."[3] The fifth is the scourges of the lashers, of which it is said, "Judgments are prepared for the scorners and striking hammers for the bodies of fools."[4] The sixth is palpable darkness without and within, of which it is said, "A land of misery and darkness where the shadow of death is"; and elsewhere, "I go to a land that is dark and covered with the mist of death";[5] and again, "They shall never see light";[6] and in another place, "The wicked shall

2 Ps. 57:11.
3 Cf. Isa. 26:10.
4 Wisd. 5:14–15.
1 Matt. 13:50.
2 Ps. 10:7.
3 Isa. 66:24.
4 Prov. 19:29.
5 Job 10:22, 21.
6 Cf. Ps. 48:20.

be silent in darkness."[7] The seventh punishment is the confusion of sinners; "For then," we read, "the books will be
opened,"[8] that is, the consciences of men will be manifest to
all. The eighth is the horrible sight of the demons, who will be
glimpsed in the movement of blazing sparks arising from the
fire.[9] The ninth punishment is the chain of fire with which each
of the limbs of the wicked is bound.

Now the first punishment of hell is for those of unbridled appetites; the second for those of malicious will; the third for the
lecherous; the fourth for the envious and those who hate; the
fifth is for those who in this world did not deserve to be beaten
with scourges, because "the sinner hath provoked the Lord, according to the multitude of his wrath he will not seek him;"[10]
the sixth is for those walking in darkness who disdainfully refused to come to the true light, namely, Christ; the seventh is for
those who confess their sins and despise repentance; the eighth is
for those who freely see the evils in this world and do them; and
the ninth is for those who have wallowed in every vice, who
travel the road of their own desires and follow only their own
appetites.

IX ·

On the Fire of Hell

The fire of hell is not fed by wood nor kindled by wind, but was
created unquenchable by God from the beginning of the world.
Thus it is written, "A fire that is not kindled shall devour him."[1]
It is thought to be under the earth, according to the prophet:

---

7 I Kings 2:9.

8 Apoc. 20:12.

9 It should be remembered that the fire of hell was said to burn but not
give light; presumably this black fire of hell could be imagined to produce
lighted sparks.

10 Ps. 10:4.

1 Job 20:26.

"Hell below was in an uproar to meet thee at thy coming."[2] But every place is one of punishment for the wicked, who always carry their torment with them and everywhere they go meet torment coming at them: "I will bring forth," he says, "a fire from the midst of thee to devour thee."[3] The fire of hell, however, will always blaze and never give light, always burn and never consume, always afflict and never go out. For there is in hell the profoundest obscurity of darkness, an immense harshness of punishment, an eternity of misery. "Bind his hands and feet and cast him into the exterior darkness; there shall be weeping and gnashing of teeth."[4]

Each member of the body will suffer torments proper to its own wrongs, so that evil-doers will be punished in those parts where they have sinned. For it is written, "By what things a man sins, by the same also he is tormented."[5] So he who sinned with his tongue was tortured in the tongue; for which he cried out, "Father Abraham, have mercy on me and send Lazarus, that he may dip the tip of his finger in water to cool my tongue, for I am tormented in this flame."[6] The finger signifies work, for we work with our fingers. It is as if to say, If I had the least work of Lazarus, I would experience less punishment.

X ·

On the Darkness of Hell

The wicked are enveloped not only in exterior but in interior darkness, because they lack spiritual as well as corporeal light. For it is written, "Away with the wicked lest he see the glory of God,"[1] who alone will be in "everlasting light."[2] The wicked,

2 Isa. 14:9.
3 Ezech. 28:18.
4 Matt. 22:13.
5 Wisd. 11:17.
6 Luke 16:24.

1 Cf. Isa. 26:10.
2 Isa. 60:19.

however, will suffer such anguish in their punishments that they will scarcely be able to think of anything because of it, but "There they direct their thoughts where they experience the force of pain."[3] Indeed, a certain student is said to have appeared after death to his teacher. When the teacher understood that the man was damned, he asked him if any Questions[4] were disputed in hell. He is said to have answered that in hell they inquire only into one thing: Whether there is anything that is not a punishment.

But Solomon says, "For neither work, nor reason, nor wisdom, nor knowledge shall be in hell, whither thou art hastening."[5] For there is among the wicked such darkness of mind, such blindness of soul, such confusion of reason, that rarely if ever are they able to rise to any thought of God, and still less to sigh in repentance. For "Praise perishes from the dead,"[6] as from one who is not. For it is written, "The dead shall not praise thee, O Lord, nor any of them that go down to hell."[7] "For hell shall not confess to thee, neither shall death praise thee."[8]

XI ·

On the Variation of Punishments

"Suffer me, therefore," said Job, "that I may lament my sorrow a little before I go and return no more, to a land that is dark and covered with the mist of death, a land of misery and darkness, where the shadow of death and no order, but everlasting horror dwelleth."[1]

There will indeed be order in the quantity of punishments,

3 Peter Lombard, *Libri Sententiae* IV. 50. 2.

4 The technical term for points of theology open to discussion in the universities.

5 Eccles. 9:10.

6 Ecclus. 17:26.

7 Ps. 113:17.

8 Isa. 38:18.

1 Job 10:20–22.

because "With what measure you mete, it shall be measured to you again."[2] So he who has sinned more grievously will be punished more grievously. "For the mighty shall be mightily tormented."[3] But there will be no order in quality: they will all be plunged from icy water into unbearable heat, so that the sudden extremes will inflict a more dread torment. For I have found from experience that if one who has been burnt applies cold, he feels a more burning pain.

XII ·

On the Despair of the Damned

"They are laid in hell like sheep; death will feed on them."[1] This text is based upon the similarity of damned souls to beasts of burden, who do not tear up the grass by the roots but only chew the top, so that the grass grows again for pasture. Thus the wicked, as if eaten by death, spring to life again to die once more, and so are eternally dying.

The liver of Tityus, unconsumed and ever growing,
Wastes not—whence it can be devoured many times.[2]

Then death will never die, and those who are dead to life will live for death alone. They will seek death and never find it, having had life and lost it. Hear what John says in the Apocalypse: "In those days men will seek death and they will not find it, and they will desire to die and death will flee from them."[3] O death, how sweet you would be to these souls who when alive thought you so bitter; they will long for you and you alone—they who had despised you so in life.

2 Matt. 7:2.
3 Wisd. 6:7.
1 Ps. 48:15.
2 Ovid, *Epistulae ex Ponto* I. ii. 42.
3 Apoc. 9:6.

XIII ·

Why the Wicked Will Never Be Released
from Punishment

Therefore let no man flatter himself, saying "The Lord will not always be angry, nor will He threaten forever,"[1] and "His mercy is over all His works."[2] For "when He was angry He did not forget to be merciful,"[3] nor does He hate anything which He has made. They take up this erroneous argument because of what our Lord said through the prophet, "And they shall be gathered together as in the gathering of one bundle into the pit. And they shall be shut up there in prison, and after many days they shall be visited."[4] And therefore—so they argue—because man sinned in time, he will not be punished in eternity.

O vain hope, O false presumption! "He shall not believe, being vainly deceived by error, that he may be redeemed with any price,"[5] "for there is no redemption in hell."[6] Therefore sinners shall be gathered in a pit and shut in a prison, which is Hell; and there they will be tortured without their bodies until Doomsday, and then after many days they shall be visited, that is, after they rise with their bodies on the last day; but they will be visited with vengeance, not salvation, for they will be punished still more grievously after the day of judgment. Thus it is said in another place, "I will visit their iniquities with a rod and their sins with stripes."[7]

Therefore God will be angry with those who are saved only for a time, for "He scourges every son whom he receives."[8] From

1 Ps. 102:9.
2 Ps. 144:9.
3 Cf. Ps. 76:10.
4 Isa. 24:22.
5 Job 15:31.
6 Resp. III Noct. *Officium Defunctorum*
7 Ps. 88:33.
8 Heb. 12:6.

this it is understood that "He will not always be angry."[9] But with the wicked He will be angry forever, for it is just and right that those who go astray in *their* portion of eternity shall have God's wrath throughout *His* eternity. For although the sinner in Hell has lost the opportunity of sinning, still he does not lose his will to sin. It is written: "The pride of those who hate thee ascends continually."[10]

The wicked will not be humbled, having already despaired of mercy. Malignant hate will grow in them, so much that they will wish God, through whom they know they exist so unhappily, could altogether cease to exist. They will curse the Almighty and blaspheme the Everlasting, complaining that He is evil who created them for punishment and never inclines to mercy. Hear what John says in the Apocalypse: "And great hail came down from heaven upon men, and men blasphemed God for the plague of the hail because it was exceeding great."[11]

Therefore the will of the damned, although it lose the effect of its power, will always retain the love of evil; it will of itself be a punishment in hell, which had been a sin in the world, though perhaps even in hell it will still be a sin, but not worth punishment.[12] Thus the sinner, having always had within himself the accusation of guilt, will always feel within himself the anguish of punishment: what he did not wipe away through penitence, God will not remit through indulgence. "Therefore it pertains to the great justice of the judge that they never lack punishment in hell who never wished to lack sin in life. They would have certainly wished, if they could, to live forever so that they might sin forever."[13] For they show that they want always to live in sin who never cease to sin while they are alive.

---

9 Ps. 102:9.

10 Ps. 73:23.

11 Apoc. 16:21.

12 Sin was said to be its own punishment because it caused anguish and frustration. See A. L. Kellogg, *Speculum*, XXVI (1951), 461 ff., for a description of St. Augustine's doctrine. The self-punishing character of sin exists in the world but does not come to full fruition until the sinner is damned and in Hell.

13 St. Gregory, *Dialogues* IV. 44.

XIV ·

Testimonies on Eternal Punishments

"Which of you," says Isaiah, "can dwell with everlasting fire?"[1]
"These shall be smoke in my anger, a fire burning all day,"[2]
"night and day it shall not be quenched and the smoke thereof
shall go up forever."[3] "And I will bring an everlasting reproach
upon you and a perpetual shame which shall never be for-
gotten."[4] "And those that sleep in the dust of the earth shall
awake, some unto life everlasting, and others unto reproach, to
see it always."[5] "When the wicked man is dead, there shall be
no hope anymore."[6]

For the wicked man damnation comes immediately and he is
destroyed at once, nor will he ever have a cure. "If any man shall
adore the beast and his image, he shall also drink of the wine of
the wrath of God and shall be tormented with fire and brimstone; and the smoke of their torments shall ascend up forever
and ever, neither have they rest day nor night, who have adored
the beast and his image."[7] Truth itself confirms this in Holy
Writ, which curses the damned in judgment, saying, "Depart
from me, ye cursed, into everlasting fire, which was prepared for
the devil and his angels."[8] If according to divine judgment "In
the mouth of two or three witnesses every word may stand,"[9] how
much more in the mouth of so many great men will *revealed*
truth stand.

1 Cf. Isa. 33:14.
2 Isa. 65:5.
3 Isa. 34:10.
4 Jer. 23:40.
5 Dan. 12:2.
6 Prov. 11:7.
7 Apoc. 14:9–11.
8 Matt. 25:41.
9 Matt. 18:16.

XV ·

On the Day of Judgment

"Behold, therefore, the day of the Lord shall come, a cruel day, and full of indignation, wrath, and fury, to lay the land desolate and to destroy the sinners thereof. For the stars of heaven and their brightness shall not display their light, the sun shall be darkened in its rising, and the moon shall not shine with her light. And I will visit the evils of the world, and against the wicked for their iniquity, and I will make the pride of the infidels to cease, and will bring down the arrogance of the mighty."[1] "Therefore shall all hands be faint, and every heart of man shall melt and shall be broken. Writhings and pains shall take hold of them, they shall be in pain as a woman in labor. Everyone shall be amazed at his neighbor, their countenances shall be as faces burnt."[2] "That day is a day of wrath, a day of tribulation and distress, a day of calamity and misery, a day of darkness and obscurity, a day of clouds and whirlwinds, a day of trumpets and alarms, for the Lord shall make a speedy destruction of all them that dwell in the land."[3] "And that day shall come upon you suddenly as a snare upon all who are on the face of the earth."[4] Because, "As lightning comes out of the east and appears even into the west, so also shall be the coming of the Son of Man."[5] "The day of the Lord shall come as a thief in the night. For when they shall say, 'Peace and security,' then shall sudden destruction come upon them, as the pains upon her that is with child, and they shall not escape."[6]

[1] Isa. 13:9–11. Innocent turns here to a third subtopic, judgment.
[2] Isa. 13:7–8.
[3] Soph. 1:15–16, 18.
[4] Luke 21:34–35.
[5] Matt. 24:27.
[6] I Thess. 5:2–3.

XVI ·

On the Preliminary Tribulation

But "great tribulation, such as has not been from the beginning of the world until now, nor shall be,"[1] will precede the judgment. "And unless those days had been shortened, no flesh should be saved."[2] "For nation shall rise against nation, and kingdom against kingdom. And there shall be great earthquakes in diverse places and pestilences and famines and terrors from heaven and tempests."[3] "And there shall be signs in the sun and in the moon, and in the stars; and upon the earth distress of nations, by reason of the confusion of the roaring of the sea and the waves, men withering away for fear and expectation of what shall come upon the whole world."[4] "For there shall arise false Christs and false prophets and they shall show great signs and wonders so as to deceive if possible even the elect."[5]

"Then the man of sin shall be revealed, the son of perdition, who opposes and is lifted up above all that is called God, or that is worshipped, so that he sits in the temple of God, showing himself as if he were God,"[6] "whom the Lord Jesus shall kill with the spirit of his mouth."[7] But "Elias the prophet will be sent before the coming of the great and dreadful day of the Lord. And he shall turn the heart of the fathers to the children, and the heart of the children to their fathers."[8] With him Enoch shall come also and "they shall prophesy a thousand two hundred

1 Matt. 24:21.
2 Matt. 24:22.
3 Luke 21:10–11.
4 Luke 21:25–26.
5 Matt. 24:24.
6 II Thess. 2:3–4.
7 II Thess. 2:8.
8 Mal. 4:5–6.

sixty days, clothed in sackcloth." "And when they shall have finished their testimony, the beast that ascends out of the abyss shall make war against them, and shall overcome them, and kill them. And their bodies shall lie in the streets of the great city where their Lord was crucified." "And after three and one-half days the spirit of life shall enter into them."[9]

XVII ·

How the Lord Shall Come to Judgment

"Immediately after the tribulation of those days, the sun shall be darkened and the moon shall not give her light, and the stars shall fall from heaven, and the powers of heaven shall be moved; and then shall appear the sign of the Son of Man in heaven. And then shall all the tribes of the earth mourn over themselves."[1] "And the kings and princes and tribunes, the rich and the strong and every bondman and freeman shall hide themselves in the dens and the rocks of mountains, and they shall say to the mountains and the rocks, 'Fall upon us and hide us from the face of him who sits upon the throne and from the wrath of the Lamb, for the great day of their wrath is come, and who shall be able to stand?'"[2] "And he shall send his angels with a trumpet and a great voice and they shall gather his elect from the four winds of heaven, from the farthest parts of the heavens to the utmost bounds of them."[3]

Then "the Lord himself shall come down from heaven with commandment and with the voice of an archangel and with the trumpet."[4] And "all who are in the graves shall hear the voice

9 Apoc. 11:3, 7–8, 11.
1 Matt. 24:29–30.
2 Apoc. 6:15–17.
3 Matt. 24:31.
4 I Thess. 4:16.

of the Son of God and they that have done good things shall come forth unto the resurrection of life, but they that have done evil unto the resurrection of judgment."[5] "Death and hell shall give up the dead that were in them,"[6] and "every eye shall see him, and they also that pierced him,"[7] "the Son of Man coming in the clouds with great power and majesty."[8]

The Lord, however, will come to judgment not only with the angels but with the senators of his people: "He is honorable in the gates when he sits among the senators of the land."[9] For they will seat themselves "on twelve seats judging the twelve tribes of Israel."[10] "I beheld," he said, "till thrones were placed, and the Ancient of Days sat. His garment was white as snow, and the hair of his head like clean wool; his throne like flames of fire, the wheels of it like a burning fire. A swift stream of fire issued forth before him, thousands of thousands ministered to him and ten thousand times a hundred thousand stood before him."[11] "God shall come manifestly, our God shall come and shall not keep silence; a fire shall burn before him and a mighty tempest shall be round about him."[12] "Clouds and darkness are round about him, justice and judgment are the establishment of his throne."[13] "He shall call heaven from above and the earth to judge his people."[14] Then "All nations shall be gathered together before him, and he shall separate them one from another, as the shepherd separates the sheep from the goats. And he shall set the sheep on his right hand, but the goats on his left."[15]

---

[5] John 5:28–29.
[6] Apoc. 20:13.
[7] Apoc. 1:7.
[8] Luke 21:27.
[9] Prov. 31:23.
[10] Matt. 19:28.
[11] Dan. 7:9–10.
[12] Ps. 49:3.
[13] Ps. 96:2.
[14] Ps. 49:4.
[15] Matt. 25:32–33.

XVIII ·

On the Power, Wisdom, and Justice of the Judge

O how great will be the fear and trembling then, how great the weeping and wailing! For if "the pillars of heaven tremble and quake at his nod,"[1] "and the angels of peace shall weep bitterly,"[2] what shall sinners be doing? "If the just man shall scarcely be saved, where shall the ungodly and the sinner appear?"[3] Wherefore the prophet cries out, "Enter not into judgment with thy servant, for in thy sight no man living shall be justified."[4] "If thou, O Lord, will mark iniquities, Lord, who shall stand it?"[5]

For who should not fear that Judge who is all-powerful, wise, and just? All-powerful, whom none can escape; all-wise, whom none can deceive; all-just, whom none can corrupt. "If strength be demanded, he is most strong,"[6] being wise of heart and powerful in strength; "If equity of judgment be demanded, no man dare bear witness for me. If I would justify myself, my own mouth shall condemn me; he shall prove me wicked although I should be simple."[7] "For he spoke and they were made, he commanded and they were created."[8] "He calls the stars and they say, 'We are here.'"[9] "Who made his angels spirits and his ministers a burning fire,"[10] whose "will nothing at all resists,"[11] "for

1 Job 26:11.
2 Isa. 33:7.
3 I Pet. 4:18.
4 Ps. 142:2.
5 Ps. 129:3.
6 Job 9:19.
7 Job 9:19–21.
8 Ps. 148:5.
9 Cf. Bar. 3:35.
10 Ps. 103:4.
11 Cf. Rom. 9:19.

whom no word is impossible,"[12] to whom "every knee shall bow in heaven, on earth, and under the earth."[13]

None can escape Him, so the prophet says: "If I ascend into heaven, thou art there; if I descend into hell, thou art present."[14] "He searches the reins and the hearts,"[15] to whose "eyes everything is naked and open,"[16] who "has numbered the sands of the sea and the drops of rain,"[17] "the Lord the God of all knowledge,"[18] foreknowing all things and aware of all things, secret scrutinizer of all secret things.

None can deceive him, so the Apostle says: "No creature is invisible in his sight."[19] He is the just judge, powerful, long-suffering, who does not swerve from the path of rectitude for "plea or bribe,"[20] neither for love or hate, but going always upon the King's highway passes no evil but he punish it, passes no good but he reward it. None can corrupt him: so the psalmist says, "Thou wilt render to every man according to his works."[21]

XIX ·
On Divine Judgment

Who would not fear that trial where prosecutor, lawyer, and judge are all the same? For He will be our prosecutor when He says, "I was hungry and you did not give me to eat, I was thirsty and you did not give me to drink."[1] He will be our lawyer when He pleads, "As long as you did it not to one of these least of

12 Luke 1:37.
13 Phil. 2:10.
14 Ps. 138:8.
15 Cf. Apoc. 2:23.
16 Heb. 4:13.
17 Cf. Ecclus. 1:2.
18 I Kings 2:3.
19 Heb. 4:13.
20 Ps.-Cicero, *Rhetorica ad Herrenium* III. iii. 4.
21 Ps. 61:13.
1 Matt. 25:42.

mine, neither did you do it to me."[2] He will be our judge when He sentences, "Depart from me, ye cursed, into everlasting fire."[3] Witnesses will scarce be needed for this judgment, because the "hidden things of darkness"[4] will then be brought to light. "Nothing is covered that shall not be revealed."[5]

Then will the books of conscience be opened, and the dead will be judged by what is written in those books about their deeds. What shame will there be for sinners! What confusion when their wickedest crimes are made manifest to all! "Blessed are they whose iniquities are forgiven and whose sins are covered."[6] No appeal can ever be made from that sentence because "the Father has given all judgment to the Son,"[7] "who shuts and no man opens, who opens and no man shuts."[8] "For the mouth of the Lord has spoken it."[9]

XX ·

That Nothing Can Help the Damned

Then will their wealth not help them, neither their honors defend them nor their friends procure them favor. For it is written, "Their silver and their gold shall not be able to deliver them in the day of the wrath of the Lord."[1] "The kings of the earth shall weep and bewail when they see the smoke of the burning,"[2] "because of fear of its torments."[3] "What then will you do in the day of visitation and calamity which comes from afar? to whom

2 Matt. 25:45.
3 Matt. 25:41.
4 I Cor. 4:5.
5 Matt. 10:26.
6 Ps. 31:1.
7 John 5:22.
8 Apoc. 3:7.
9 Isa. 58:14.

1 Ezech. 7:19.
2 Apoc. 18:9.
3 Apoc. 18:15.

will you flee for help?"[4] "Everyone shall bear his own burden."[5] "The soul that sins, the same shall die."[6]

O strict judgment!—not only of actions, but "of every idle word that men shall speak, they shall render an account";[7] payment with the usurer's interest will be exacted to the last penny. "Who hath showed you to flee from the wrath to come?"[8]

"The Son of Man shall send his angels and they shall gather out of his kingdom all scandals, and them that work iniquity, and they will bind them as bundles to be burnt, and shall cast them into the furnace of fire. There shall be weeping and gnashof teeth,"[9] there shall be groaning and wailing, shrieking and flailing of arms and screaming, screeching and shouting; there shall be fear and trembling, toil and trouble, holocaust and dreadful stench, and everywhere darkness and anguish; there shall be asperity, cruelty, calamity, poverty, distress and utter wretchedness; they will feel an oblivion of loneliness and namelessness; there shall be twistings and piercings, bitterness, terror, hunger and thirst, cold and hot, brimstone and fire burning, forever and ever world without end.

Here endeth the book of Lothario
on the misery of the human condition.

---

4 Isa. 10:3.
5 Gal. 6:5.
6 Ezech. 18:20
7 Matt. 12:36.
8 Luke 3:7.
9 Matt. 13:41–42.

SELECTED BIBLIOGRAPHY

EDITION

Michele Maccarrone (ed.). *Lotharii Cardinalis (Innocentii III) De miseria humane conditionis*. Lugano: *Thesaurus Mundi*, 1955.

BIOGRAPHY

Leonard Elliott-Binns. *Innocent III*. London: Methuen & Co., 1931.

Achille Luchaire, *Innocent III*. 6 vols. Paris: Librairie Hachette, 1906–1908.

Charles Edward Smith. *Innocent III: Church Defender*. Baton Rouge, La.: Louisiana State University Press, 1951.

Helene Tillmann, *Papst Innocenz III*. Bonn: Ludwig Röhrscheid Gmbh., 1954.

BACKGROUND

Friedrich Kempf. *Papsttum und Kaisertum bei Innocenz III*. Rome: Pontifica Università Gregoriana, 1954.

Michele Maccarrone. *Chiesa e Stato nella dottrina di Innocenzo III*. Rome: Lateranum, 1940.

Sidney R. Packard. *Europe and the Church under Innocent III*. New York: H. Holt and Co., 1927.

James M. Powell (ed.). *Innocent III: Vicar of Christ or Lord of the World?* Boston: D. C. Heath and Co., 1963. [Collection of readings with bibliography.]

"CONTEMPT OF THE WORLD": INTELLECTUAL HISTORY

Robert Bultot. *Christianisme et valeurs humaines: La doctrine du mépris du monde,* IV, tomes 1 and 2. Louvain and Paris: Nauwelaerts, 1963–1964. [Other volumes to follow.]

Willard Farnham. *The Medieval Heritage of Elizabethan Tragedy*. Berkeley, Calif.: University of California Press, 1936; reprinted, Oxford: Blackwell, 1956.

Donald R. Howard. *The Three Temptations: Medieval Man in Search of the World*. Princeton, N.J.: Princeton University Press, 1966.

Charles E. Trinkaus, Jr. *Adversity's Noblemen: The Italian Humanists on Happiness*. New York: Columbia University Press, 1940.

PERTINENT ARTICLES

Robert Bultot, "Mépris du monde, misère et dignité de l'homme dans la pensée d'Innocent III," *Cahiers de civilisation médiévale,* IV (1961), 441–456.

Donald R. Howard, "Hamlet and the Contempt of the World," *The South Atlantic Quarterly,* LVIII (1959), 167–175.

Robert Enzer Lewis, "Chaucer's Artistic Use of Pope Innocent III's *De miseria humane conditionis* in the Man of Law's Prologue and Tale," *PMLA,* LXXXI (1966), 485–492.

Michele Maccarrone, "Innocenzo III prima del pontificato," *Archivio della R. Deputazione di Storia Patria,* LXVI (1943), 59–134.

Revue d'ascétique et de mystique, XLI (1965), 3: a collection of articles under the general title "La notion de 'Mépris du Monde' dans la Tradition Spirituelle Occidentale."